MARCO  POLO

C000152379

ISRAEL

May this
travel
inspire you
and give you
the strenght to carry on
changing the world -
        I love you,
                matey

The best Insider Tips → p. 4

INSIDER TIP

Best of ... → p. 6

The Mediterranean Coast → p. 32

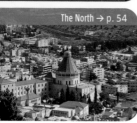

The North → p. 54

SYMBOLS

INSIDER TIP   Insider Tip

★   Highlight

●●●●   Best of ...

☀   Scenic view

☺   Responsible travel: fair trade principles and the environment respected

PRICE CATEGORIES HOTELS

Expensive   over 500 shekel

Moderate   250–500 shekel

Budget   under 250 shekel

The prices are for two people in a double room including breakfast

PRICE CATEGORIES RESTAURANTS

Expensive   over 200 shekel

Moderate   125–200 shekel

Budget   under 125 shekel

The prices are for a three-course meal without drinks

On the cover: Saved from demolition by Dadaists p. 43 | Romantic campfires in the Negev p. 89

CONTENTS

Jerusalem→ p. 64

The South → p. 86

Trips & Tours → p. 106

Road atlas → p. 120

DID YOU KNOW?

MAPS IN THE GUIDEBOOK

(122 A1) Page numbers and coordinates refer to the road atlas
(0) Site/address located off the map. Coordinates are also given for places that are not marked on the road atlas
(U A1) refers to the street map of Jerusalem inside the back cover

INSIDE BACK COVER: PULL-OUT MAP →

PULL-OUT MAP 𝄞

(𝄞 A–B 2–3) Refers to the removable pull-out map
(𝄞 a–b 2–3) Refers to additional inset maps on the pull-out map

The best MARCO POLO Insider Tips

Our top 15 Insider Tips

INSIDER TIP A life's work for the memory of others
The Lohamei Hagetaot Kibbutz near Akko preserves the history of survivors of the Warsaw Ghetto in films, photographs and books → p. 36

INSIDER TIP Ocean view and sea breeze
The vibrant restaurant Boya at Tel Aviv's old harbour combines unique culinary delights with art and culture → p. 48

INSIDER TIP Among critical friends
The NGO crowd gets together to smoke hookahs in the atmospheric Kkan Zaman bar in the Jerusalem Hotel on Nablus Road, East Jerusalem → p. 79

INSIDER TIP Art Deco Hotel Neve Tzedek
Guests can spend the night near the beach in Tel Aviv's historical Neve Tzedek district in this lovingly restored small hotel of the same name → p. 51

INSIDER TIP Israel's finest youth hostel
The Karei Deshe youth hostel is located on the shore of the Sea of Galilee surrounded by palm trees and luxuriant greenery and without much of the normal youth hostel atmosphere. The perfect place to rest your weary head → p. 60

INSIDER TIP Where the Sermon on the Mount took place
You can wander in Jesus' footsteps in Tabgha north of the Sea of Galilee und clamber up the Mount of the Beatitudes. This is where Jesus first said the Lord's Prayer. The view is magnificent → p. 61

INSIDER TIP In a climatic health resort
It is only a few miles from Jerusalem but seems to be in a completely different world and one that is worth exploring. Ramallah, the health resort and seat of the Palestinian President, is experiencing a boom and you will enjoy the cafés and restaurants lining the streets → p. 84

BEST OF ...

FOR FREE

● *Drumming at sunset*
In Tel Aviv, not-so-devout Israelis welcome the Sabbath in their own way. They get together for a drumming session on the beach and give a free concert lasting for two hours → p. 40

● *Guest at a baptism*
Want to watch several baptisms at the same time? The *Kinneret Kibbutz* on the Sea of Galilee invites you to take part in impressive, perfectly organised baptism ceremonies free of charge → p. 100

● *Keep your eye on the government*
Heated discussions on the future of the country often take place in the *Knesset*, Israel's parliament in Jerusalem. Wouldn't you like to experience what you normally only see on the news in real life? The politicians quarrel in Hebrew but there are free guided tours in English → p. 81

● *In the oldest section of Tel Aviv*
You can learn a lot just by taking a stroll through *Old Yafo*. This is all made possible on a free tour held every Wednesday to make visitors aware of the history and everyday life of this district → p. 47

● *Almost like an open-air museum*
The Jerusalem district of the 'hundred doors' *Mea Shearim* has preserved the flavour of shtetl life in Eastern Europe in the 19th century and has now developed into something of an open-air museum of Orthodox Judaism. Visitors are welcome as long as they are modestly dressed and observe the Sabbath regulations (photo) → p. 74

● *Garden stroll*
The most perfect gardens in Israel are in Haifa. They belong to the Baha'i and climb the terraces on Mount Carmel. Flower lovers will not only enjoy the splendour of exotic blossoms as they walk along the well-cared-for gravel paths on their free tour but also magnificent views of the Old City wherever they stop → p. 38

●●●● Dots in guidebook refer to 'Best of ...' tips

● *In the Kibbutz*
The first Zionist settlers founded the first kibbutzim 100 years ago. Today, these communities are very popular as guesthouses – one of them is *En Gev* on the Sea of Galilee → p. 61

● *Kosher, of course*
Even sceptics will be convinced about how tasty kosher cooking can be in *Café Batia* in Tel Aviv. It received the rabbinate's prized certificate not in a competition among top chefs but as proof that they prepare all their food faithful to the laws of the Bible → p. 48

● *Tracing the stories in the Bible*
In no other country can you come as close to the events described in the Bible as in Israel. Visit the *Basilica of the Annunciation* in Nazareth where it is reported that Mary received the news that she would soon give birth to Jesus → p. 57

● *The Sabbath at the Western Wall*
Shortly before sunset on Friday, crowds of pious, solemnly dressed, Jews flock through the Old City of Jerusalem to the *Western Wall*. They welcome their holy day with intense prayers; you are permitted to watch but photography is not allowed on the Sabbath (photo) → p. 73

● *'The Wall'*
If you walk along the 8m (25ft)-high *security wall* of cement in the El Tur district of Jerusalem, you can witness many artistic and political graffiti on the 'canvas' of history erected to separate the West Bank → p. 76

● *Heroic epic*
Visitors reach the fortress of *Masada* either up the 'snake path' or by cable car. Here, a spectacular son et lumière explains why this place, which represents the myth of heroic Judaism for the State of Israel, 'shall not fall again' → p. 93

● *Three religions – one country*
In *Wadi Nisnas* in Haifa you will be able to experience how the different religions live together and celebrate Christmas, Hanukkah and Ramadan with each other → p. 40

ONLY IN

BEST OF ...

● *Visit the philharmonia*

The world-renowned Israel Philharmonic Orchestra plays under Zubin Mehta regardless of the weather – and not only in the evening. It is advisable to reserve tickets on-line for the concerts in the *Frederic Mann Auditorium* → p. 50

● *Underground*

The Christian crusaders expanded the harbour city of *Akko* to a fortress and used it for 200 years for their supplies from Europe. Today, you can explore the Templar's magnificent ceremonial halls and subterranean battlements (photo) → p. 35

● *Shop 'til you drop*

Off to the shopping malls – they provide a cool atmosphere to escape Israel's heat! The three-storey *Jerusalem Mall* has a wide range of high-class fashion shops including famous international brands. You will need a break from time to time to regain your strength → p. 78

● *Experience history*

You will lose track of time in the *Israel Museum*, the country's largest and most important museum, in Jerusalem. Especially recommendable: the exhibition of old Bible texts from Qumran and the scale reconstruction of Jerusalem in the Roman period → p. 72

● *Fun with underwater friends*

Experience the wonderful sea world in the *Underwater Observatory Marine Park* in Eilat. Sharks and turtles also swim their laps here. If you want it even more interesting, take a glass-bottom boat and cruise through the submarine world → p. 91

● *Inside a work of art*

Do you feel like walking in the footsteps of the Romans, going on a pleasant exhibition tour or just relaxing in a restaurant? All of this is possible under a single roof in the architecturally fascinating *Castra* in Haifa → p. 38

HEAT

RELAX AND CHILL OUT
Take it easy and spoil yourself

● *Surrounded by peace in the madness of Jerusalem*
A small sign on the edge of the gravel path reminds visitors to be quiet. You will feel the power of peace in the *Garden of Gethsemane* and the Church of All Nations where one should also not speak → **p. 75**

● *Forget that sinking feeling*
Lie on the water and float without having to move and without going under; that is the unique experience in the *Dead Sea* 400m (1300ft) below sea level (photo) → **p. 95**

● *Spa time in Jerusalem*
Even in the holiest of cities, the body still needs to be taken care of. The *American Colony Hotel* offers the perfect possibility for those wanting to enjoy therapeutic herbal infusions and be massaged with fragrant oils → **p. 80**

● *Emotional moments in Tiberias*
The beach promenade *Tayyalet* is romanticism in its purest form! Sitting on the shore of the Sea of Galilee with a breathtaking panoramic view of the Golan Heights and the slowly setting sun with a few small boats bobbing up and down on the water – who would want to be anywhere else? → **p. 59**

● *Over the roofs of Jerusalem*
Bid farewell to the day listening to the call of the muezzin on the roof of the exquisite Vatican pilgrims' hostel opposite Jerusalem's Old City. Enjoying wine and cheese in *Roof Top*, you will feel as if time has come to a standstill → **p. 78**

● *Sunbathing in Tel Aviv*
The day on the beach in Tel Aviv begins as soon as the joggers disappear in the morning. The long beach is painstakingly cared for and, if you prefer, it is even possible to relax and enjoy sunbathing with other members of your own sex only → **p. 50**

INTRODUCTION

DISCOVER ISRAEL!

Israel: the country of sunny holidays, of educational tours loaded with culture and archaeological excursions, the country of rapt pilgrimages, the Bible and the Lord, the centre of the world's main religions and their sacred sites. And, the country where Palestinians and Israelis have irreconcilably insisted on their 'rights' for 60 years and made it the starting point and centre of the Middle East conflict.

Israel is a small country, almost exactly the same size as Wales. Its excellent roads make it easy to get around and they also make it possible for visitors to take their time reaching their destination. Most visitors' first impression of Israel is the arrival hall of the Ben Gurion Airport in Lod. Here – and even more so in Tel Aviv 23km (14mi) away – one experiences the modern Israel and does not recognise any fundamental differences to other metropolises in the western world. But, even in Tel Aviv, you will feel the flair of the Orient, smell unfamiliar aromas, see scenes that appear to come from the East. The beach along Lahat Promenade is completely European, the beach fashions are the same as in Rimini or on Ibiza – only 'topless' is disapproved of.

Photo: Haifa, view to the Baha'i shrine

Witnesses to history: ancient olive trees in the Garden of Gethsemane on the Mount of Olives

Regardless of whether your beach holiday is on the Mediterranean coast or in Eilat on the Red Sea, it would be a pity to limit your stay in this country to just swimming and sunbathing. In any case, a trip 'up to Jerusalem' at an altitude of 800m (2600ft) in the Mountains of Judea is a must. If you drive there in the early evening and see the sun setting behind Jerusalem and the long shadows it casts creating even stronger contours on the barren limestone hills on both sides of the road, you will feel the tranquillity that is so appropriate to 'Al Quds', 'The Holy' – as the Arabs call Jerusalem. The best time to wander through the Old City is in the morning when it is slowly coming to life. The proprietors of the Palestinian bazaars can be seen arranging their wares, pious Jews at the Western Wall greet the day with 'Hear O Israel, the Lord is one God', Franciscan monks in their brown habits hurry to the Church of the Holy Sepulchre and young Israeli soldiers patrol the narrow streets.

Profound religiosity, the conviction of being 'chosen' by God, Yahweh or Allah, the certainty of being in possession of the One Truth, seems to separate people more than unite them. This can be felt at many places in Israel and that not only between the

1500BC
Pastoral tribes move from Mesopotamia (now Iraq) to Palestine

957BC
King Solomon builds the First Temple in Jerusalem

587BC
King Nebuchadnezzar II destroys the First Temple. The period of so-called 'Babylonian Captivity' begins

70AD
The Roman Emperor Titus destroys the Second Temple. Following this, the area of Palestine is controlled for centuries by the powers dominating the Middle East

three monotheistic religions but also within the individual communities. Jerusalem is the culminating point of all of the chaos in the Middle East. The dignitaries of two dozen Christian churches have their residences in the Christian quarter of the Old City alone and visitors from the west are often confronted with the great variety of Christianity here for the first time.

It is less a matter of confessional variety than the everyday dispute over the right religious lifestyle on earth that leads to differences among the Jews. Visitors can also be drawn into this conflict, especially on the Sabbath in the Mea Shearim district of Jerusalem where they will be confronted with a form of Jewish life that they only thought existed in literary depictions of shtetels in Eastern Europe. Although Mea Shearim appears to be something of an exotic enclave, Jewish fundamentalism is very influential in Israel. In the country's political life, the religious parties have often tipped the scales and the Chief Rabbinate makes sure that today's Jewish lifestyle is in line with the rules of the Torah.

You will hardly feel anything of the political and religious movements in the city once you get away from the big towns – in the north of Galilee, for example. The landscape there is characterised by cypresses and olive trees. Here, in the north, the Sea of Galilee lies 200m (650ft) below sea level surrounded by mountains, and its water is used today to irrigate the Negev Desert. The Jordan leaves the lake not far from the Deganya kibbutz, the first to be founded in Palestine, before making its 100km (62mi) journey to the Dead Sea.

> **The Sea of Galilee also irrigates the Negev**

Today, the Jordan is effectively the eastern border of Israel seeing that, after the conquest of the Palestinian West Bank in the Six Day War, the Kingdom of Jordan starts at the river of the same name. Jericho is located at the southern end of the Jordan Valley. Before Ramallah, it was the administrative capital of the future Palestinian state until 1999. It is only a one-hour drive from Jericho to Jerusalem where you can still feel 3000 years of history in the Old City. If you take a walk along the city wall erected by Sultan Suleiman in 1540, you will discover many of the sites in and outside the Old City: Jerusalem is the most historically important city in Israel. This is also where the most devastating period that led to the founding of the State of Israel is also remembered. The memorial to the Holocaust, Yad Vashem, confronts its visitors with documents that are almost impossible to bear. In Israel, people often ask how such a monstrous thing was possible and why so few people had enough courage to rise up against it. There can be no 'compensation' for this genocide and everybody today should be responsible for taking decisive action against any form of contempt for human beings and nationalistic pathos – worldwide, but especially at home and in Israel.

> **Jerusalem has been formed by 3000 years of history**

In the early 1990s, it appeared that peace might have a chance in the Middle East. Simon Peres, Yitzhak Rabin and Yassir Arafat were awarded the Nobel Peace Prize for drawing up an agreement intended to lead to two independent states that would recognise the sovereignty of each other. But then Yitzhak Rabin was murdered by a Jewish fanatic on 4 November, 1995. Under Prime Minister Ariel Sharon, the situation escalated due to suicide attacks carried out by individual Palestinians and Israel's construction of a concrete wall between Israel and the West Bank, partly on occupied territory in the future Palestinian state in breach of international law. The Israeli withdrawal from the Gaza Strip in the same year took place too late to be considered a gesture of peace. Since then, Gaza has been ruled by the radical Hamas in confrontation with Yassir Arafat's successor who was elected in 2005, Mahmoud Abbas, with his administration in Ramallah. There have been many peace attempts since the first talks in Oslo in Norway 20 years ago, but all have failed on account of Israel's claim on territory going beyond the 1967 borders. The Israeli settlements on the West Bank

1979	1987	1993	1995	After 2001	2005
Sinai returned to Egypt (Camp David Agreement)	Revolt of the Palestinians in the occupied areas (1st Intifada)	Gaza Jericho agreement	Yitzhak Rabin murdered; peace process comes to a halt	2nd Intifada, Palestinian suicide attacks	Evacuation of the Gaza Strip. Israel builds the wall – partly on Palestinian territory

The Monastery of the Temptation on a rock high above the Palestinian town of Jericho

have played a significant role in this matter. In 2011, the American President Obama spoke publically about this border as part of a two-state solution for the first time. In this way, the USA approached the demands made by the United Nations. With these targets set by Israel's protector the USA, it appears possible that peace now has a better chance.

However, there are still many hurdles on the path to peace. And, it can be very difficult for visitors to discuss this extremely sensitive matter with Israelis, to ask questions, not to express a personal opinion but listen to those of the people living in the country. You will have

> **How close is peace?**

no problems going on a carefree hike with members of the Israeli Nature Protection society, living in a kibbutz or taking part in a dig at an archaeological excavation. And, you will frequently also meet Israelis who are very open – and sometimes even critical about their country.

2008
War in the Gaza Strip

2009
Benjamin Netanyahu elected Prime Minister

2010
The construction of settlements on the West Bank, in breach of international law, stops for a time

2011
Start of the 'Arab Spring'. Egypt's President Mubarak deposed, opening of border to the Gaza Strip. Palestine applies for UN membership

2012
Orthodox Jews protest in Jerusalem for gender separation in public transport

WHAT'S HOT

1 Kosher and good

Nouvelle cuisine Traditional dietary rules and modern cooking don't have to contradict each other. Chef Kobi Dellal proves this in his gourmet restaurant *Tokopaya (Hapatish 6, Tel Aviv)*. His colleagues in the *Meatos* Grill Restaurant also know how to handle the commandments and conjure up food that is full of flavour *(Weizmann 2, Tel Aviv www. meatos.co.il)*. The focus in *Deca* is on Mediterranean gourmet cuisine: pure heaven! *(Ha Ta'asiya 10, Tel Aviv, deca.reste.co.il)*

On a rope

2

Downhill Even abseiling rookies make good progress on the impressive rock formations in the country. Secured by a rope and wearing a helmet, you can make your way down from the top of the canyon. The adventurous then continue on down the river; for example with the team from *Eretz Hatzvi Events (www.israel-al. com*, photo). Other abseil professionals are *www.ashdot. info, www.israelextreme.com* and *www.israel-outdoor-adventures.com* that offer tours throughout Israel.

See you again

3

Recycling *Yoav Kotik* makes jewellery out of crown corks and tins *(www.kotik-design.com*, photo), old plastic bags are the raw material for Inbal Limor's sculptures and Merav Feiglein uses all kinds of discarded objects – from toothbrushes to plastic dolls – for her works of art. The trend to make art out of waste can be seen everywhere. Those interested in finding out more about Recycle Art can take a tour with Merav Feiglein or lay down a 'litter mosaic' in her studio *(Givat Shapira, www.meravart. com)*. Bosmat Niron is another artist who recycles for her work and creates practical articles such as outdoor furniture out of old bottles *(www.bosmatniron.com)*.

Literature to go?

4

For bookworms Multitasking is hot in Israel's cafés. In more than 200 establishments, guests can choose something more substantial from the menu to go with their coffee. Coffeehouses not only serve coffee, they also sell second-hand books. The project called 'Same Old Story' has developed into an enormous success — especially because the guests of the cafés not only buy but also exchange books *(re-books.org.il, photo)*. One of the cafés that jumped on the bandwagon is the charming *Muskat* that also sells fashion and designer objects *(HaDekel St, Udim, www.muskat.org.il)*. Ilan's House of Coffee has branches all over the country where fair trade products and literature make a good match *(Ibn Gvirol St 90, Tel Aviv, www.ilans.co.il)*.

Very fashionable

5

Tel Aviv look The lively metropolis on the sea inspires up-and-coming designers: extravagant cuts and materials, way-out combinations and new interpretations hang on the racks here. And they are not only wearable — they are also affordable! This is true of the fashion designed by Helena Blaunstein alias *Frau Blau (Ha'Hashmal 8, www.fraublau.com, photo)*. *Tovale's* not only satisfies fashionable women, it also clothes their offspring. That is where little girls get to feel like a princess *(Dizengoff St 220, www.tovale-s.com)*.

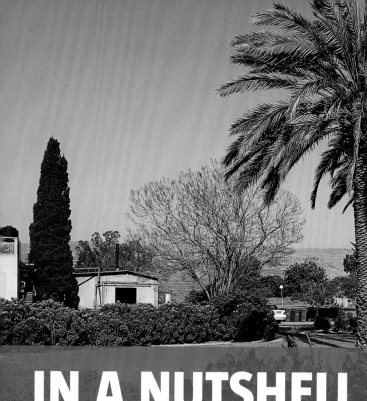

IN A NUTSHELL

DEAD SEA

This large salty sea at the lowest point on the earth's surface that became famous as the Dead Sea is changing dramatically. Its level falls by around 2.3ft every year. If nothing is done to alter this, the Dead Sea will cease to exist in 300 years. If you drive along the shore of the sea, the changes become apparent immediately. Spas and bathing establishments that used to attract people with skin and respiratory ailments with their location directly on the shore are now much further inland and far away from the beach. The drop in the water level creates a small step-like terrace on the shore every year. It forms in winter when the rain compensates for the losses and the level remains the same for a few months during which time the waves erode the shore. This happens year after year and, for this reason, the Sea has sunk and its surface area reduced by a quarter. Today only a trickle of water from the Jordan River water, which both Israel and Jordan need for drinking and agriculture, finally reaches the Dead Sea. Discussions on a solution have been underway for years and involve a pipeline from the Mediterranean or a canal from the Red Sea. But so far nothing has happened because of the high costs involved.

Photo: Kibbutz on the Sea of Galilee

Kibbutzim, the languages, the Dead Sea –
a small lexicon with names, facts and terms
to help you understand the country better

ERETZ ISRAEL

Israel's claim to the Occupied Territories is justified only by the fact that God promised the Jews *Eretz Israel* (Genesis 13, 14–17, 15, 18–21) as far as the River Jordan. There are actually hardly any important Jewish religious sites within Israel's pre-1967 'green' border, most of them being in the areas conquered in 1967. Internationally, there is considerable opposition to Israel's argumentation using the Torah as a kind of land register.

GAZA JERICHO AGREEMENT

Israel and the PLO signed an agreement in Washington on 13 September, 1993 designating Palestinian partial autonomy for the Gaza Strip and sections of the West Bank. The world at large interpreted this agreement as the first step towards a Palestinian state. But Israel is delaying its withdrawal. The 'roadmap' agreed on in 2002 is also still waiting to be fulfilled. So far, a retreat has taken place from less than one quarter of the West Bank.

GOVERNMENT

Israel is a parliamentary democracy. The Prime Minister and 120 members of

INTIFADA

Intifada comes from the Arabic word for 'to rise up, shake off'. The Palestinians in the occupied areas stood up against the Israeli military occupation with strikes and stone-throwing between 1987 and 1993 (1st Intifada). The goal was the creation of an independent Palestinian state. This officially came to an end with the signing of the Gaza Jericho agree-

Rabbi studying in the shade of the Western Wall

the parliament *(Knesset)* are elected for four years by all Israelis without any division into constituencies. As neither conservative parties *(Likud, Kadima)* nor the Labour Party *(Marach)* have ever reached an absolute majority, the small – usually religiously oriented – parties have considerable influence on political events. The head of state (Simon Peres, since 2008) is elected by the Knesset for a five-year term. Since 2009, Israel's present Prime Minister, Benjamin Netanyahu, has led a coalition of right-conservative and politico-religious parties.

ment. However, Israel's halting withdrawal and its continuing to build settlements on the West Bank led to the 2nd Intifada. It initially targeted Israel as an occupying force but then Palestinian suicide attacks began in the Israeli mother country. According to Israeli newspapers, 1036 Israelis and 3592 Palestinian died during the Second Intifada. Mahmoud Abbas and Ariel Sharon official put an end to the 2nd Intifada at the beginning of 2005. Since 2007, Hamas does not feel itself bound to this agreement in the Gaza Strip.

JUDAISM

'Every Jew has the right to immigrate to Israel' and, since 1952, every Jewish immigrant ('returner') automatically becomes a citizen. Non-Jews are not permitted to immigrate. Who is a Jew? Official definition: 'Anybody with a Jewish mother or who has converted to Judaism and does not belong to any other religion is a Jew.' The aim of the State of Israel is to develop a population structure with a single cultural and religious background. Judaism is founded on the *Talmud* (Hebrew: study, teaching) the compendium of Jewish religious regulations composed in the 6th century that includes the *Torah*, the Hebrew collective name for the Five Books of Moses in the Bible. They are considered to be the word of God.

The Jews in Israel can be divided into the communities of the *Ashkenazim* (Jews from West and East Europe as well as the USA whose cultural and social life follows European patterns) and the *Sephardim* (all Jews with an Afro-Asiatic background). Irrespective of these groups, secular and orthodox Jews confront each other in Israel; especially the ultra-pious *Haredim* (no military service, only study of the Holy Scriptures, many children) are increasing their political influence.

KIBBUTZIM

Jews who migrated to Palestine after 1909 developed a new kind of agricultural undertaking as the realisation of Socialist ideals of equality and in the interest of political security: shared life, shared income and shared upbringing of the children. Currently, only around three percent of Israelis live on a kibbutz; many kibbutzim now run small hotels. *www.kibbutz.org.il*

LANGUAGES

The official languages in Israel are Hebrew, the reactivated and updated language of the Jews, and Arabic. English is understood everywhere in the country. Hebrew names are transcribed phonetically and are merely an attempt to transfer the sounds and intonation of the Hebrew word into the respective second language. That is why you will often find the same word written in many different ways in Roman letters. The term for 'New Year', for example can be written as *Rosh Ha Shana* or *Rosh Hashanah*. The transcription closest to English is frequently used. There is an increasing tendency to use Hebrew exclusively for information and on street signs.

MIDDLE EAST CONFLICT

In 1917, the British Foreign Minister Lord Balfour publicly assured Baron Rothschild of the 'establishment of a national homeland for the Jewish people in Palestine'. On the other hand, the British High Commissioner in Egypt, Sir Henry McMahon, had already promised the Hashemite Great Sharif of Mecca to support and recognise an independent Greater Arabia after the fall of the Ottoman Empire, to which the Palestine and Arab population living there formally belonged until 1918. After 1918, Great Britain forgot both of its promises and took over Palestine itself as a mandated territory of the League of Nations until 1948. The proposal put forward by the UN in 1947 for a confederative solution with two states and Jerusalem as an internationalised city did not come to fruition as a result of the rejection on the part of the Arab states and proclamation of the State of Israel by the Jewish population of the mandate. Since then, armed hostilities have characterised the Israeli-Palestinian conflict resulting in mass expulsion in 1948 and large territorial changes in 1967. Today, there are still Palestinian refugee camps under the care of the UN in neighbouring Arab states and Israel still holds the areas it conquered in 1967 (East Jerusalem and the Golan Heights) annexed or, in the case of the West Bank, under military occupation for 60 years. A peaceful solution to the Middle East conflict is not in sight. Although the reasons are complex, most people on both sides consider that the best way to peace in the Middle East lies in the creation of two states. The recognition of Palestine as an independent state by the UN would not solve the Middle East conflict overnight, but it would increase the impetus of the movement towards peace after decades of inertia.

OCCUPIED TERRITORIES

Israel has occupied the Syrian Golan Heights and the major portion of the West Bank – the area to the west of the River Jordan that used to be part of the Kingdom of Jordan but which the country renounced for the benefit of a Palestinian state – since its military victory in 1967. However, according to international law, permanent military occupation after a victory is illegal and this fact is regularly condemned by the United Nations. Israel withdrew from the Gaza Strip, which it had occupied for close to 40 years, in 2005. So far, the Palestinians only administer certain sectors (so-called A Zones) autonomously. These are cities such as Hebron, Nablus, Ramallah and Jericho on the West Bank that are isolated from each other and which Israeli forces can invade at any time.

PALESTINIANS

The Palestinians are an Arab people without a territory of their own. After Jewish settlers in the British mandate proclaimed the independent State of Israel in sections of historical Palestine in 1948, and Jordan, Syria and Egypt took over the rest after the subsequent Middle East War that was fought as a result of this, Israel was quickly recognised by the UN while the demand for an independent Palestinian state has remained the core of the conflict in the Middle East to this day.

As a consequence of their history, the national rights of the Palestinians have so far not been continuously represented politically. The British mandate administration ran the country from 1920–1948; after that, sections were administered by Jordan and Egypt and the territories have been occupied by Israel since 1967. The Gaza Jericho Agreement of 1993 made it possible for them to establish autonomy on their own territory for the first time.

Today, almost 1.2 million Palestinians live as a minority group in Israel with an additional 1.9 million on the West Bank and about 1.3 million in the Gaza Strip. A further 800,000 are in refugee camps in Syria and Lebanon and 300,000 have emigrated to work in other Arab countries. It is estimated that 40–65 percent of the 3 million inhabitants of Jordan are Palestinians.

Over time, the political goals of the Palestinians and their main political representative body, the Palestine Liberation Organization (PLO), under the leadership of Yassir Arafat (1929–2004) have changed. Until 1967, the aim was to establish a secular state in the territory of the British mandate of Palestine in armed combat but, after the Rabat Conference in 1974, the focus was turned towards the creation of an independent Palestinian state on the territory of the Gaza Strip and the former Jordanian sections on the West Bank. The fundamentalist Hamas increased its influence when the success of the Oslo Peace Treaty failed to materialise.

At the beginning of 2005, Mahmoud Abbas was elected President of the Palestinians. In 2006, his party – *El Fatah* – won parliamentary elections but Hamas was

The *Shrine of the Book* preserves the oldest Biblical texts

victorious in the Gaza Strip: Since then, their anti-Israel position has intensified (e.g. by firing rockets into Israeli territory). Israel's response has been the bombardment and isolation of the Gaza Strip.

POPULATION

Today, 6.8 million citizens with an Israeli passport live in the territory of the State of Israel (within the borders of 1948 and 1967 recognised by international law). Around 5.3 million are Jewish and 1.5 million non-Jewish Israelis including 1.2 million Moslems, 130,000 Christians as well as 90,000 Druzes. The more than 300,000 Jewish settlers on the Palestinian West Bank and about 200,000 Jews who now live in annexed East Jerusalem are also Israelis. In addition to the Druzes, approximately 7000 Jewish Israelis live on the annexed Syrian Golan Heights. More than one third of Israel's Jews were not born in the country but are immigrants.

TEMPLES

The Temple in Jerusalem was the scene of many biblical events and the centre of the Jewish faith. The First Temple was built by King Solomon around 950BC and totally destroyed by King Nebuchadnezzar in 563BC. After their return from captivity in Babylon, the Jews started to build a new temple on the same site in 538BC. This Second Temple was destroyed by the Romans in 70AD; the only section to have been preserved to this day is the Western Wall that is most commonly referred to as the 'Wailing Wall'.

ZIONISM

Zion is the symbolic Biblical denomination for Jerusalem and Israel. The First Zionist World Congress, organised by Theodor Herzl in Basel in 1897, formulated the notion of a homeland in Palestine for Jews scattered throughout the world. This 'Return to Zion' was fulfilled by the proclamation of the State of Israel in 1948. Today, the realisation of *Eretz Israel* and, with it, the annexation and settlement of the West Bank is fundamental to the concept of political Zionism.

FOOD & DRINK

A unique Israeli cuisine, completely different from that of any other nation, does not exist. The inhabitants and cooks in the country still prepare food the way their parents did, and they came from more than 80 countries and brought their local dishes with them to Israel.

This means that you can eat excellent French or Yemenite, Moroccan or Austrian, Russian or Polish, Argentinean or Hungarian food – always pepped up with a touch of the Orient.

The Israeli breakfast is really sumptuous. Most hotels and cafés provide a mammoth buffet with fresh fruit, eggs cooked in countless ways, many different types of cheese, olives and vegetable salads, *humus* and yoghurt, as well as smoked and marinated fish, topped off with the usual bread rolls and jam.

Lunch is a good time to try out some Oriental specialities. Israelis often begin a meal with *mezze*. The word can be translated as starter, snack, hors d'œuvre or *amuse geule* but none of these terms can do full justice to the wide variety of – boiled, simmered or raw – food served in small bowls that are placed on the table in front of the guests: stuffed wine leaves and *humus,* chicken liver and pickles, onion rings in vinegar, pickled turnips, *tabbouleh* and olives and *zhoug* (chilli paste

Photo: Beach restaurant, Eilat

All the specialities of the Orient – visitors to Israel can enjoy kebabs, humus and excellent wines

with parsley and coriander), to name just a few. Everybody takes what he or she wants – from the bread basket as well. People who put a little bit of everything on their plate at once give themselves away as tourists. Israelis take one dish after another in order to be able to fully savour each delicacy.

Many dishes mentioned in the Bible have lost none of their importance in Israel today. The different varieties of bread made exclusively of wheat, barley, millet and rye are very important. The round *Rosh Ha Shanah bread* symbolises happiness, the *Sabbath bread* is a plaited loaf, the size of the *Challah* bread depends on the specific holiday. *Pita bread* made of wheat flour, salt, yeast and a little bit of oil accompanies many dishes. The keyword 'kosher' is falsely connected with Jewish

LOCAL SPECIALITIES

▶ **Blintzes** – sweet pancakes filled with cream cheese or farmer cheese

▶ **Falafel** – deep-fried balls of humus; often served with salad in pita bread

▶ **Gefillte fish** – fish farce with many different ingredients either stuffed in a fish skin or served in the shape of a fish

▶ **Hamentashen** – triangular cookies filled with jam, syrup or sugar icing; a Purim speciality

▶ **Humus** – a creamy chick-pea puree seasoned with lemon juice, garlic, cumin and sesame paste. In the morning, with warm pita bread, at lunchtime and in the evening with garlic and lemon juice to accompany boiled beans, with fresh salad and olives (photo left)

▶ **Kebab** – grilled or fried, balls of spicy, minced beef or lamb

▶ **Knish** – a kind of dumpling filled with onions, potatoes and seasoned meat

▶ **Konafa** – pastry with honey syrup, almonds, nuts and pistachios

▶ **Krupnik** – a thick soup with barley, beans, vegetables and meat

▶ **Mashi** – stuffed aubergines

▶ **Matzo** – unleavened bread

▶ **Matzo balls** – dumplings made of matzo bread, milk and salt – sometimes in breadcrumbs and fried; served at the Purim feast

▶ **Schischlik** – skewered roast lamb or beef

▶ **Seniya** – lamb or beef *tahini* sauce (*tahini* is a creamy fat made of white sesame seeds)

▶ **Shawarma** – roast lamb or chicken freshly sliced from a revolving spit and served in pita bread

▶ **Cholent** – East European bean stew with potatoes and fatty meat

▶ **Tabbouleh** – Salad of bulgur, with a great deal of parsley, mint and lemon juice (photo right)

cooking and appears on every menu in Jerusalem. In Hebrew, kosher means pure, clean, permitted, and defines whether the ingredients used in the dishes and their preparation conform to the religious concepts of the Old Testament. All restaurants have a sign stating whether they are kosher or not. According to Moses, the meat of any animals with 'divided cloven hoofs' and which 'chew their cud' – goats, cattle and sheep – is permitted. Pigs and camels do not fulfil these requirements.

Slaughtering according to Jewish rights, with the complete bleeding of the animal, is the only acceptable method. Rabbits, wild birds and marine animals 'with neither scales nor gills' are considered unclean. Lobsters, mussels, crabs and eel have therefore not found their way onto the kosher menu. You will never find meat with a cream sauce in a kosher restaurant; according to the Jewish dietary laws *(kashrut),* there must be a strict separation of meat and milk in the preparation and this means there must also be at least a six hour time span between consuming them. It is against religious laws to drink coffee with milk after you have eaten a meal with meat. To be completely sure, kosher restaurants and strictly orthodox families have two separate kitchens and different pots, crockery and cutlery for meat and dairy products.

Israelis are very fond of fish and like to grill it, seasoned with garlic, lemon juice and paprika, over charcoal. Israel meets all of its own needs through coastal and deep-sea fishing and from fish farms. Even the famous John Dory – also known as St Pierre or Peter's fish – which is offered everywhere around the Sea of Galilee because this is where Saint Peter and the other Disciples cast out their nets, no longer comes from there.

Probably the first fish dish that comes to mind when one thinks about the art of Jewish cooking is *gefillte fish.* This is an indefinable, pressed mass of fish, beneath a thick, gelatinous sauce; a kind of pâté that smells like – and is served in the shape of – a fish. The dish almost certainly originated in Poland. For centuries, Polish Jews had the custom of attempting to stabilise the form of cooked fish, which often fell to pieces, using a jelly-like sauce of sugar and almonds.

Compared to the Arab dinner, the Israeli meal is usually a comparatively light affair.

Today, there is no need to go without the Arabic cuisine served in good restaurants in East Jerusalem and in all of the other major cities in the country. Israeli Palestinians and Jews from Arab countries have preserved their culinary art.

The Rothschilds are responsible for it being possible to drink excellent local wines in Israel today. In 1886, Baron Edmond gave Zionist settlers on the western slopes of Mount Carmel several wine presses. The climate and soil were perfectly suited to viniculture and Jews were able to produce kosher wine for their religious celebrations in the Promised Land for the first time in 2000 years. Today, the *Carmel Winery* in Zikron Yaakov is the largest of

Israel also produces excellent wines

the more than 200 wine-growing enterprises in Israel. For the past four decades, wine has also been grown on the mountains in Galilee and on the (Syrian) Golan Heights, annexed by Israel, and exported to many countries.

Informal clothing is all that is required for a restaurant visit – even in elegant establishments. Smoking is forbidden in all restaurants.

SHOPPING

The range of goods in Israel is hardly any different from that in European countries, especially seeing that special articles are usually imported from Europe or the USA. Prices in elegant shops on *Dizengoff* (Tel Aviv) and *King David* and *Ben Yehuda Streets* (Jerusalem) are similar to Europe. However, diamonds and jewellery and, in many cases, furs and leather goods are cheaper than in Europe. But bear the EU customs regulations in mind when you return home.

DEAD SEA COSMETICS

The Dead Sea has the world's highest concentration of minerals. Many natural elements that are important for the health and smoothness of the skin can be found in its layers of mud. Cleopatra, who visited the Dead Sea as a spa to enhance her beauty more than 2000 year ago, is often cited as a testimonial to the effectiveness of Dead Sea Cosmetics. As *A'Hava*, they set out from the *Mizpe Shalem Kibbutz* on the shore of the Dead Sea near En Gedi and have now conquered the world. There is an especially large

selection of A'Hava lotions and creams at reasonable prices in Israeli perfume shops *(www.deadseacosmetics.com)*.

DEVOTIONAL OBJECTS

The largest selection of Christian gift articles and biblical souvenirs can be found in the old city of Jerusalem and around the Sea of Galilee. Their unique advantage: they are made in the Holy Land.

JEWELS

The most diamonds and every third precious stone produced in the world are processed in Israel – and then exported. The world's largest jewellers – first and foremost, Stern and Oppenheimer – have subsidiaries in Israel and the branches in the luxury hotels will give you a first impression of the wealth VIPs flaunt.

MARKETS & BAZAARS

There are large open-air markets in almost every city. The *Carmel Market* (vegetables, fruit, and clothing) and the artists' market

You will find it hard to resist the gems, leather goods and cosmetic products from the Dead Sea, as well as the bazaars and markets

on *Nahalat Binyamin* in Tel Aviv are two of the most famous. Tourists are attracted by the bazaars in the old section of towns and villages; those traditional quarters where the same goods, in the same quality, are sold in several shops or stands next to each other. Bargaining is an absolute must in any bazaar. The largest bazaar is in the old city of Jerusalem.

FURS & LEATHER

If you are an expert, it is possible to buy furs and leather goods relatively inexpensively in Israel. Jewish furriers have a long tradition.

SHOPPING CENTRES

Impious Tel Aviv is the fashion trendsetter in the Holy Land. They do things differently there than in religious Jerusalem. Israel's answer to New York's Greenwich Village is *Sheinkin Street* in Tel Aviv. Young artists and craftspeople offer their creations in all styles and trends in small shops with antique and futuristic, oddball and kitsch articles as well as any number of cafés, restaurants and clubs in between. If this is the kind of shopping you like, you will also find what you are looking for in *Tel Aviv Port* in the former, completely revamped, harbour in the north of the city.

TYPICAL SOUVENIRS

What can I take back home? In the 'not so expensive' category: freshly picked Jaffa oranges, Carmel wine (from 'God's vineyard'), INSIDER TIP chunks of salt from the Dead Sea, an olive branch (not necessarily broken off a tree in the Garden of Gethsemane) and fresh oriental spices from one of the bazaars.

THE PERFECT ROUTE

IN AND AROUND JERUSALEM

Israel shows its many contrasting aspects in ❶ *Jerusalem* → p. 64. That is why any visit to Israel should begin with this exciting city where the most important religious places of worship of the three monotheistic world religions are located just a stone's throw away of each other. If you take time and drink tea in a café in the old city, you will soon come into contact with the locals. Detours to the nearby Palestinian towns of ❷ *Bethlehem* → p. 83 and ❸ *Ramallah* → p. 84 will make you aware of the everyday difficulties resulting from the never-ending conflict in the Middle East.

INTO THE JORDAN RIVER VALLEY

Leaving Jerusalem, you travel almost 1200m (4000ft) down to the Dead Sea in the Jordan Valley where ❹ *Qumran* → p. 94, the place where the oldest Biblical texts were found, lies waiting for you in the south (photo left). En route, after you pass the oasis of ❺ *En Gedi* → p. 92, that today welcomes many visitors as a kibbutz, nature park and spa you will be able to assail ❻ *Masada* → p. 93. Wandering through the ruins on a cliff 400m (1300ft) above the valley, and trying to imagine how things were during the Roman siege, is one of the most lasting impressions of any trip to Israel.

TO THE SEA OF GALILEE

You turn around in Masada and follow the Jordan River from the end of the Dead Sea to the north until you reach ❼ *Jericho* → p. 84, one of the oldest cities in humanity. The journey then continues via ❽ *Bet Shean* → p. 61 to ❾ *Tiberias* → p. 58. The ❿ *Sea of Galilee* → p. 62, 200m (650ft) below sea level, is just another of the many highlights in Israel (photo right). Visitors who make a tour around the lake pass the most important places where Jesus was. In ⓫ *Kefar Haruv* → p. 63 you will be able to get a feeling for the strategic importance of the Golan Heights. This is also an ideal place for anybody who likes surfing.

Experience the many facets Israel has in store, from Jerusalem to the Red Sea, with a stopover on the shores of the Sea of Galilee

IN GALILEE

After leaving the Sea of Galilee, you head through the valleys and mountains of Galilee to the northwest of Israel and the town of **12** *Nazareth* → p. 55. Since Jesus' time, light wine has been grown on some of the slopes in the vicinity and can be tasted in the restaurants in town. The route now takes us to the Mediterranean Coast and **13** *Akko* → p. 34, where the age of the Crusaders can still be felt.

ON THE MEDITERRANEAN

Israel's almost 200km (125mi)-long Mediterranean coast stretches from the chalk cliffs at **14** *Rosh HaNiqra* → p. 37 near the Lebanese border north of Akko to the Gaza Strip in the south with many large and small seaside resorts and Israel's largest port **15** *Haifa* → p. 37 south of Akko in between. The city has a very beautiful 'German Colony' where the pavement cafés will tempt you to take a break. The Romans left their mark on the Mediterranean coast as archaeology fans will discover in **16** *Caesarea Maritima* → p. 52 The modern city of **17** *Tel Aviv* → p. 43, is located in the middle of Israel's coastline; it offers something for all tastes – and that, day and night.

THROUGH THE DESERT

A beach holiday in Eilat on the Red Sea is the perfect way to end a visit to Israel. Those in a hurry can take a plane from Tel Aviv but if you really want to experience the country you should drive. In four hours, your route will take you along the coast via Ashdod and Ashkelon on a fascinating

890km (550mi); Driving time: 15 hours
Recommended time for this trip:
10–17 days. Detailed map of the route
on the back cover, in the road atlas and
the pull-out map

tour through Israel's largest desert, the Negev, then on to **18** *Beersheba* → p. 86 and into the Jordan Valley with the bathers' paradise **19** *Eilat* → p. 90 at its southern end.

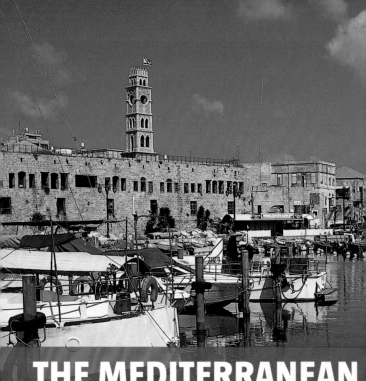

THE MEDITERRANEAN COAST

Israel's coastline between Lebanon and the Palestinian-administered Gaza Strip measures exactly 187km (116mi), the longest stretch of any country in the eastern Mediterranean region. Today, the small and large beach resorts from Nahariya in the north to Ashkelon in the south offer those seeking relaxation and sun worshipers everything they could possibly desire.

There are beautiful, clean sandy beaches with a perfect infrastructure for tourism, all sorts of interesting destinations for excursions into the hinterland that show just how important this stretch of coast was historically, and a variety of hotels and other forms of accommodation in all price categories.

Tel Aviv, Israel's largest city and economic centre, is located almost exactly in the centre of the coast close to the most important airport in the country near Lod that is named after the founder of the state David Ben-Gurion. This is where most visitors first set foot in the Holy Land. But, it was not always like that. The importance of the cities on the Mediterranean coast – Akko and Ashkelon, Caesarea and Haifa – was originally founded on their harbours through which conquerors and pilgrims, swarms of immigrants and plundering crusaders made their way into Palestine.

Photo: Akko

The Mediterranean coast was once the gateway for merchants and conquerors – today, it is the site of Israel's most beautiful beaches

The fertile Plain of Sharon between Tel Aviv and Haifa – or, more exactly, between Mount Carmel in the north and the Yarkon River in the south – is often referred to as the granary of Israel. This is where Israel is most densely populated. An infrastructure comparable with that of large cities in Europe can only be found in the Tel Aviv metropolitan area. This is where the gem cutting industry settled, where trade flourishes and where the most money is made. Nowhere else in Israel are the road network and transportation links as dense as they are on the coastal plain.

In Antiquity, the the busy and most important trade and transportation route in the eastern Mediterranean area – the Via Maris – passed through this plain on the coast of Israel.

Once a resting place for travellers and their camels: the caravanserai Khan el Umdan

AKKO (ACRE)

(122 B2–3) *(𝓜 D3)* **Situated at the north-ern end of the Bay of Haifa, Akko (pop. 60,000) is one of the oldest harbour cities on the Mediterranean and held the same importance for the Romans, Christian crusaders and Moslems.**

Its architecture from the various periods of its history makes it possible for today's visitors to get an idea of its historical significance. In 2001, the Unesco added the Old Town of Akko to the list of World Heritage Sites.

We know from the Bible that this was the place where Paul – the city was called Ptolemais at the time – made a stop on his travels. It served the Romans as a garrison town and they built the first surfaced road from here to Antioquia. In 1104, the crusaders under Balduin I made it their harbour in the Holy Land but this was also where their Palestinian adventure came to an end in 1291. In the 18th century, while under Ottoman rule, Akko made historical headlines one last time: Ahmed al-Jezzar, who had carried out a major building programme in Akko, thwarted Napoleon's attempts to capture the city.

Akko is one of the few cities in Israel with a predominantly Palestinian population and it has preserved its Arab character to this day. The main places of interest from the period of the crusades are in the walled Old Town; ancient Akko *(Tel El-Fukhar)* is around 3km (1¾mi) to the south.

SIGHTSEEING

EL JEZZAR MOSQUE

The El Jezzar Mosque is the Arab symbol of the city. Ahmed al-Jezzar ('the slaughterer') had it built on the ruins of the Holy Cross Church between 1780 and 1790. However, this mosque is not famous for its austere Islamic architecture but for the 'beard of the Prophet' that is sometimes still referred to today when oaths are made. One of the hairs of the Prophet's beard is preserved here and is showed to the faithful on the 27th day of Ramadan every year. The cells where Koran students used to live can be seen in the cloisters around the inner courtyard of the mosque. There is also a small domed building, shaded by trees, with the sarcophaguses of El Jezzar and his adoptive son Suleiman who followed him as governor. *Daily (except at prayer times) 6am–5.30pm | entrance fee 10 NIS*

KHAN EL UMDAN

There was a great demand for accommodation in Akko. One of these large hotels – the columned caravanserai – was built by Ahmed el-Jezzar in 1785. The stables were located around the large collonaded inner courtyard with the rooms for those staying there in the galleries on the upper floor. Sultan Abed el Hamir II had the high clock tower added in 1906. *Old Town, at the fishing harbour | entrance free*

CRUSADER CITY ★ ●

Akko's most important sight is located beneath the ground: the well-preserved fortified city of the crusaders. The Knights of St John developed the harbour into the military metropolis of the crusaders' realm and, in this way, assured the supply of provisions from Europe for the Kingdom of Jerusalem they had founded. The crypt lies under the massive citadel, built by Ahmed el-Jezzar in the 18th century, which can be seen from far away. It served as a dining and ceremonial hall. A number of wide corridors fan out from here to other rooms in the fortress and a 65m-long tunnel leads to the Knights Templar's pilgrim hospital. In 1994, a more than 350m-long *Templars' Tunnel* was discovered by chance

when a blocked water pipe was being repaired. This tunnel, cut into the rock and the walls later vaulted with hewn stone, leads directly to the harbour. During the time of the British mandate, the fortress was used as a gaol where members of the Jewish underground movement were imprisoned and executed. This period is documented in the *Museum of Heroism. Sat–Thu 8.30am–6pm (in winter 5pm), Fri 8.30am–5pm | opposite the El Jezzar Mosque | entrance fee 45 NIS*

FORTIFICATIONS

The crusaders fortified Akko from the land and sea sides with a massive wall and several watchtowers that the Ottomans then renovated in the 18th century for

★ **Crusader city**
The subterranean city of the Knights of St John in Akko
→ p. 35

★ **German Colony**
19th-century commune at the foot of Mount Carmel → p. 39

★ **Rondo Grill**
Dinner in the restaurant of the luxurious Hotel Dan Carmel in Haifa → p. 41

★ **Caesarea Maritima**
The aqueduct is the most impressive ruin in the Roman city → p. 52

★ **Baha'i Gardens**
The most beautiful garden complex in Israel: the splendour of blossoming geometry on the slopes of Mount Carmel → p. 38

MARCO POLO HIGHLIGHTS

their own protection. The following three towers are particularly impressive:

The *Burj el Kommandor* at the northeastern corner with 'Napoleon's cannon' (which was actually cast in Belgium long after Napoleon's death) protected the city to the land side; from here, a path led along the wall to the old harbour and Argaman Beach.

The ☆ *Burj Kureijim*, the northwestern tower, strengthened the city wall on the side open to the sea; from here, the wall runs to the south to *Burj el Kishla* and further to Burj el Sanjak.

The *Burj el Sanjak* in the southwest is the section of the fortifications that protrudes the furthest into the sea and is also the most massive. It belonged to the Templar Order, served as a lighthouse and safeguarded the harbour.

FOOD & DRINK

The atmosphere makes the restaurants on the marina right below the city walls especially attractive: *Abu Christo | tel. 04 9 91 00 65, Ptolomeus | tel. 04 9 91 61 12,* or the excellent fish restaurant in the courtyard of the lighthouse overlooked by the Burj Sanjak *Abu Christo | tel. 04 9 55 22 12; all daily 11am–10pm | Moderate*

WHERE TO STAY

AKKOTEL

Small boutique hotel near the city wall, around 50m from the marina, with a charming rooftop terrace. *16 rooms | Salahudin St. 1 | tel. 04 9 87 71 00 | www. akkotel.com | Moderate*

ARGAMAN MOTEL

This not-so-new hotel complex is located directly on the beach on the road to Haifa. Swimming pool. *75 rooms | Seashore | tel. 04 9 91 66 91 | Moderate*

INFORMATION

ACRE OLD CITY DEVELOPMENT
Visitors Center | Weizmann St. 1 | tel. 04 9 91 21 71, 04 9 95 67 00 | www.akko.org.il

WHERE TO GO

INSIDER TIP **LOHAMEI HAGETAOT**
(122 B2) (*𝄞 D3*)

Lohamei Hagetaot (Lohamé HaGeta'ot) is a must for historically and politically interested visitors to Israel. This kibbutz, approx. 8km (5mi) to the north of Akko was founded by people from the Warsaw Ghetto who escaped death. As their life's work, they invested a huge amount of effort into establishing a historical museum dealing with the persecution and annihilation of Jews in the Third Reich. Some 40,000 photographs, 60,000 books and about 240 films, as well as drawings created in concentration camps, have been assembled in the *Ghetto Fighters House Museum. Sun–Thu 9am–4pm, Fri 9am–1pm | www.gfh.org.il | entrance fee 30 NIS*

MONTFORT ☆ (122 C2) (*𝄞 E2*)

The ruins of what was once one of the largest crusaders' fortresses, a gigantic bulwark on the approach to Akko, can still be seen from afar. Montfort, 24km (15mi) northeast of Akko, was built by the Grand Master of the Teutonic Order Hermann von Salza in 1228 as Starkenburg Fortress. It was spared the fate of being conquered – it fell, without a fight, to Sultan Beibar in 1271. Monfort was never destroyed in fighting but, over the centuries, the fortress has fallen into ruin and even partly collapsed.

NAHARIYA (122 B2) (*𝄞 D3*)

Nahariya (Nahariyya, pop. 51,000; 9km/6mi north of Akko) was founded in 1934 by Jewish immigrants who had managed

The beach at Nahariya: it is not often as deserted as this

to escape from Germany and rapidly developed into a popular holiday resort. Wide boulevards, charming shops, a very beautiful beach and large, comfortable hotels – Nahariya is probably the 'most European' seaside resort in Israel.

The River Ga'aton flows through the town; the Hebrew word for river 'naher' gave Nahariya its name. But as early as 1500BC, the Canaanites erected a temple here near the beach *(Kamaaniter St)*. A *Byzantine mosaic floor*, which was excavated with financial support from the German twin town of Bielefeld, proves that the location must have also been lived in during the first centuries after Christ.

Moshav Nes Ammim is located near Nahariya. It was founded by Dutch and German Christians in 1960 to create a place ('a signal for the peoples', Isaiah 11:10) where Christians and Jews could come together after the Holocaust. There is an excellent guesthouse here made even more attractive by a large swimming pool. *(48 rooms, 13 flats | tel. 04 9 95 00 00 | www.nesammim.com | Moderate).*

ROSH HANIQRA (122 B2) *(ᗰ D2)*

Rosh HaNiqra is located 18km (11mi) to the north of Akko near the Lebanese border; in ancient times its strategic significance as a gateway for foreign armies led to it being known as the 'ladder of Tyros'. There is a wonderful view over the Mediterranean and far inland from the 80m (260ft)-high ☼ chalk cliffs that dominate the landscape. A cable car takes visitors to the impressive grottos with their bizarre erosions below the chalk cliffs.

HAIFA

(122 B3) *(ᗰ D3)* **Israel's largest harbour lies on a beautiful semi-circular bay directly where Mount Carmel and the Mediterranean meet.**

Almost all of Israel's export activity passes through Haifa's port (Hefa) and this is also where passengers on cruise ships visiting Israel disembark. Its location on a slope means that the city (pop. 300,000) rises up the Biblical mountain on three

CITY **WHERE TO START?**

Ha Carmel: you have the best view over the city of Haifa from the Ha Carmel district. A lovely footpath leads visitors to the *Baha'i Gardens* and adjacent *German Colony (15 mins.)*. Haifa has an excellent network of public buses *(5 NIS)* that also run on the Sabbath. They make it possible to reach the museums in the lower part of town quickly *(lines 37a, 24, 36)*.

levels: the Old Town and harbour complex are at sea level, the modern commercial and administration centre *(Hadar Hacarmel)* at an altitude of around 100m (328ft) with the ☼ Har *Hacarmel* district, with many villas and expensive hotels, at about 300m (984ft) above sea level. From here – where the only underground in Israel *(Carmelit)* also has its terminus – you will have a magnificent view of the city and entire bay. On the other hand, the slope made it difficult to get through the city quickly and a toll tunnel *(11.40 NIS for two transits)* was opened in 2010 that now enables drivers coming from the south (from the Tel Aviv direction) to avoid inner-city traffic jams. 'Dazzling by day, sparkling at night, the jewel on the Mediterranean' is how the city promotes itself.

SIGHTSEEING

BAHA'I SHRINE

Bab, the forerunner of Baha'ullah the founder of the Baha'i religion, was executed in Persia in 1850 and his mausoleum with the golden dome and a magnificent park, the ★ *Baha'i Gardens*, completed in 1953, has become a city landmark. It was declared a World Heritage Site in 2008. *Daily 9am–noon (take your shoes off!), Baha'i Gardens daily 9am–5pm | Hatzionut Ave. | entrance free to both* There is a fascinating, free ● panoramic tour from Carmel down to the shrine. *Daily 9am–noon | the tour begins to the west of the observation platform at Yeve Nov St. 45 | www.ganbahai.org.il/en*

INSIDER TIP **CASTRA** ●

The Roman settlement of *Castra* was once located on the western slopes of Mount Carmel in what is now the urban area of Haifa. Today, Castra is the name of a large arts mall with dozens of arts and crafts shops, galleries and a museum with the finds from Roman excavations on two floors. The building is a work of art in its own right. The Austrian artist Arik Brauer decorated its façade with magnificently coloured majolica showing 20 scenes from the Old Testament. *Sun–Thu 10am–10pm, Fri 10am–3pm, Sat after the end of Sabbath until 10pm | Moshe Flieman Rd 4 | www.castra.co.il*

CLANDESTINE IMMIGRATION AND NAVAL MUSEUM

This museum is a house full of exciting stories but also full of suffering. One of the exhibits is the 'Af-Al-Pi', the ship that ran the blockade during the period of the British mandate to bring Jewish immigrants into the country. *Sun–Thu 8.30am–4pm | Derekh Allenby 204 | entrance fee 10 NIS*

DAGON SILO (BEIT HADAGON)

The cultural history of bread is depicted in this 70m (230ft)-high grain silo. All aspects of what people once had to go through to create their daily bread, from the earliest varieties of grain, its storage and processing to silo construction are shown. *Tours by appointment; tel. 04 8 66 42 21 | Kirkar Plumer, at the harbour | entrance free*

ELIJAH'S CAVE

Elijah, the Old Testament prophet, lived in a relatively spacious gallery (around 40m/130ft long, 8m/26ft wide and 5m/16ft high) beneath Mount Carmel in the south (today, below the Baha'i gardens). As Germans, their descendants celebrated the Nazis rise to power in the 1930s and were subsequently expelled by the British. The almost 30m-wide main street of their

Baha'i Shrine: the symbol of Haifa has been a World Heritage Site since 2008

of the city before his encounter with the false prophets of Baal (1 Kings 18: 20–40). According to one of the many legends, the cave also served as a dwelling for Joseph and the Virgin Mary. *Sun–Thu 8am–5pm (July/Aug to 6pm), Fri 8am–noon | Derekh Allenby 230 | free admission*

GERMAN COLONY ⭐

In 1869, German Christian Templers (not to be confused with the Knights Templar) from the southwest of Germany emigrated under the leadership of their ministers Christoph Hoffmann and Georg Hardegg and established a pious country community at the foot of Mount Carmel settlement with typically German stone houses (some of them with Biblical inscriptions) is known today as Ben Gurion Boulevard with cafés, restaurants and arts and crafts shops leading up to the Baha'i Gardens.

HAIFA MUSEUM OF ART

The art museum displays paintings and sculptures by contemporary Israeli and foreign artists; in addition, visitors can see archaeological and ethnological exhibits from the Mediterranean area, as well as old musical instruments. *Sat–Wed 10am–4pm, Thu 4–7pm, Fri 10am–1pm | Shabtai Levi St. 26 | entrance fee 35 NIS*

MADATECH –
NATIONAL MUSEUM OF SCIENCE

The museum of technology in the historical Technion Building invites visitors to experiment with its more than 600 exhibits. *Sun noon–6pm, Mon–Wed 10am–6pm, Thu 10am–8pm, Fri and Sat 10am–6pm | Shmaryahn Levin Hadar Hacarmel St. 25 | www.madatech.org.il | entrance fee 60 NIS*

NATIONAL MARITIME MUSEUM

A museum on 5000 years of seafaring, mainly in the Mediterranean area. Model ships, marine instruments, nautical charts and archaeological finds are on display. The museum was founded by a Jewish captain in 1955. *Mon–Wed 10am–4pm, Thu 4–9pm, Fri 10am–1pm, Sat 10am–3pm | Derekh Allenby 198 | free admission*

INSIDER TIP **RUBEN AND EDITH HECHT MUSEUM**

An absolutely first-class archaeological exhibition including an ancient wooden freight barge 'excavated' by marine archaeologists in neighbouring Nasholim Kibbutz. There are also many paintings, including works by such famous artists as Claude Monet and Vincent van Gogh. *Sun, Mon, Thu 10am–4pm, Tue 10am–7pm, Fri 10am–1pm, Sat 10am–2pm | University of Haifa | free admission*

STELLA MARIS CARMELITE CONVENT

This was founded in 1206 in the time of the crusades by Prior St Brocard and managed to survive throughout the Middle Ages during periods of both decline and reconstruction. Napoleon used it as military hospital during his siege of Akko in 1799. The basilica and a collection of exquisite antiques are particularly worth seeing. *Daily 8.30am–12.30pm and 3pm–6pm | Derekh Stella Maris | free admission*

INSIDER TIP **WADI NISNAS** ●

Wadi Nisnas is characterised by several oriental streets where Jewish and Arab Israelis have lived peacefully alongside each other for decades; sit in one of the many small restaurants and watch the colourful hustle and bustle of everyday life on the streets. In Wadi Nisnas, Chanukah and Christmas are celebrated jointly in December, as well as Ramadan at the appropriate time. *Khouri St and Yochana Hakadosh St.*

LOW BUDGET

▶ Every Friday in the late afternoon, two dozen leisure-time drummers join forces behind the former Dolphinarium on the beach of Tel Aviv and give a free two-hour ● sunset session. A kiosk provides the audience with inexpensive drinks.

▶ Bicycles are an alternative way to get around in Tel Aviv quickly. Bikes can be hired from: *Cycle Bike Rental | Ben Jehuda St. 147 | bike: 60 NIS/day*

FOOD & DRINK

CAFÉCAFÉ ☺

Healthy treats in the German Colony. The café uses many organic products. The friendly service is another good reason for a visit. *Daily 7am–10pm | Ben Gurion Blvd. 2 | tel. 04 7 03 33 07 | Budget*

CAFÉ PEER

Cheerful café and restaurant. *Closed Sat | Hanassi Ave. 130 | tel. 04 8 43 82 33 | Budget*

RONDO GRILL ★ 〰

Restaurant in the luxurious Dan Carmel Hotel with excellent international cuisine prepared using local products and with an unparalleled view from Mount Carmel down to the sparkling lights of the city and harbour – a combination that appeals to all the senses. *Closed Fri | Hanassi Ave. 85–87 | tel. 04 8 30 30 60 | Expensive*

SHOPPING

The shops that are of most interest to tourists are on *Havenim Street* near *Solej Boneh Square*.

CITY TOURS

'THE PATHS OF 1000 STEPS' 〰

The topography of Haifa makes it unavoidable that large sections of paths in the city can only be reached up or down steps but these tell conceal interesting historical details. The *Haifa Tourist Board* has picked up on this and created four special routes, each marked in a separate colour and fully signposted.

All four start from the mountain station of the Carmelit Railway or bus 22 on *Yefe Nof Street*. And you should be in good shape if you want to tackle one of these routes because they all have more than 1000 steps! The 'Historical Route' (blue) begins in the 18th century and ends at *Paris Square*; the 'Nostalgic Route' (yellow) takes guests to Haifa's German Colony; the 'Folklore Route' finishes up in *Wadi Nisnas* and the 'Classical Route' ends in front of the *House of Mustafa El Halil Pasha*.

ENTERTAINMENT

CINEMATEQUE

This is a large entertainment and amusement centre with a café that is almost

When night falls: view of glittering Haifa from Mount Carmel

always full, a cinema and a meeting place for artists. *Hanassi Ave 142*

WHERE TO STAY

BETH SHALOM

Small hotel at the top of Mount Carmel, with a cafeteria. *30 rooms. | Hanassi Ave. 110 | tel. 04 8 37 74 81 | www.beth-shalom.co.il | Moderate*

INSIDER TIP ▶ COLONY HOTEL HAIFA

Lovingly restored historical house in the German Colony below Baha'i Gardens. You will feel at home in this family-run hotel. *40 rooms | Ben Gurion Blvd. 28 | tel. 04 8 51 33 44 | www.colony-hotel.co.il | Moderate*

The 5000-year-old fortress hill of Megiddo comprises 21 layers of settlements

DAN CARMEL ☼

The first hotel of Israel's largest chain DAN is located high up on Mount Carmel. There are wonderful views of the bay from all the rooms. Hotel guests can enjoy the restaurants, swimming pool, fitness centre and sauna. *219 rooms | Hanassi Ave. 107 | tel. 04 8 30 30 30 | www.danhotels. com | Expensive*

DAN GARDENS HAIFA ☼

Small hotel on Mount Carmel with all imaginable comforts and a beautiful terrace with a magnificent view. *31 rooms | Yeve Nof St. 124 | tel. 04 8 30 20 20 | www. danhotels.com | Expensive*

DAN PANORAMA HAIFA ☼

Also on Mount Carmel because the view is like in a fairy tale. High-rise hotel with its own club for children (Danny Land) ensures families can enjoy a relaxing holiday. *266 rooms | Hanassi Ave. 107 | tel. 04 8 35 22 22 | www.danhotels.com | Expensive*

CARMEL YOUTH HOSTEL

In the southern section of the city. *16 rooms each with 5 beds | Tzivia Veltzhak St., north of Haifa Tunnel | tel. 04 8 53 19 44 | haifa@ iyha.org.il | Budget*

INFORMATION

HAIFA TOURIST BOARD

Ben Gurion Ave. 48 | tel. 04 8 53 56 06 | Sun–Thu 9am–5pm, Fri 9am–1pm, Sat 10am–3pm | www.tour-haifa.co.il

WHERE TO GO

BET SHEARIM (122 C4) (𝑀 D4)

After the Bar Kochba revolt – the last uprising of the Jews against the Romans (132–135) – the seat of the Jewish court, Bet Shearim (Bet She'arim) became one of the most important Jewish burial sites (20km/12½mi southeast of Haifa). Its discovery in 1936 was a near-miracle: a sheep had escaped from a shepherd and got lost in a crevice that turned out to be the entrance to the realm of the dead. Excavations revealed catacombs with hundreds of sarcophaguses from the 3rd and 4th centuries. *April–Sept daily 8am– 5pm, Oct–March 8am–4pm*

CARMEL (122 B3–4) (*∅ D3–4*)

Mount Carmel, a 30km (19mi)-long range of high hills southeast of Haifa, is referred to in the Bible as the 'God's vineyard'. Baron Edmond de Rothschild started growing wine here again. Today, his *Carmel Winery* in Zikron Yaakov and the neighbouring *Tishbi Estate Winery* provide Jewish communities throughout the world with kosher wine.

DRUZE VILLAGES (122 B4) (*∅ D4*)

With a population of 13,000, Daliyat El Carmel (Daliyat el Karmil), 16km (10mi) southeast of Haifa, is the largest Druze settlement in Israel. Information on Druze traditions and history can be found in the *Druze Heritage House.* Many shops sell Druze souvenirs. In 2003, the town and the Druze village of Isfiya further to the south were merged with the city of Haifa.

INSIDER TIP EN HOD
(122 B4) (*∅ D4*)

An idyllic oasis to peaceful life on the western slopes of Mount Carmel. En Hod, 15km (9mi) south of Haifa, is now an artists' colony. It was an Arab village until 1948 but was almost completely destroyed during the War of Independence. Marcel Yanco, a famous Dadaist, prevented it being razed to the ground and saved the village for Israeli artists. Today 180 families live here and organise their everyday life collectively. *Yanko Dada Museum and Galleries Sat–Thu 9.30am–5pm, Fri 9.30am–4pm*

MEGIDDO (122 C4) (*∅ D4*)

The Unesco World Heritage Site Megiddo (Tel Megiddo) is around 5000 years old and is located on the ancient Via Maris 34km (21mi) to the southeast of Haifa. Judea was defeated by the Egyptians in the battle of Megiddo in 609BC. The excavations, including the stables of Kings Solomon and Ahab, date back to biblical times. There is a model of the complex in the information centre. *Daily 8am–5pm (Oct– March to 4pm) | www.parks.org.il | entrance fee 35 NIS*

TEL AVIV

(122 A–B6, 124 B–C1) (*∅ C–D6*) **Tel Aviv is the Holy Land's worldly centre – the most modern metropolis in the Middle East. Its skyline is characterised by the skyscrapers and luxury hotels along the beach, and dazzling neon signs underline the city's importance as Israel's commercial centre.**

At the same time, Tel Aviv is also the cultural heart of the country. Nowhere else is their such a wide variety of entertainment, nowhere else are there so many galleries, cinemas, clubs and discos and as much 'worldly' life as in Tel Aviv with

---

CITY WHERE TO START?

Dizengoff Square: the centre of Tel Aviv lies between *Dizengoff Street* and the beach promenade *Haryakon*. Old Jaffa is just a short walk to the south, the new entertainment district *Tel Aviv Port* a little to the north; the 'in' places on *Sheinkin St* are only 15 mins. away on foot. The city has an excellent public bus network *(separate bus lane | fare 5 NIS)*. Taxis are expensive (European prices!) and a hired car will only cause problems because of the lack of parking spaces.

its more than 1 million inhabitants. This is where it all happens, this is where trends are set. The DJs in the clubs in *Tel Aviv Port* and on *Sheinkin Street* determine which hits are 'in' in Israel. When peace settles over the rest of the country on Friday evening, a contrast programme gets under way in Tel Aviv: 'Shabbat Night Fever'. This includes public beach parties and shopping malls that are open until midnight.

Tel Aviv is only 100 years old. In 1909, Jews from Yafo (Jaffa), which is now a district within Tel Aviv, moved to the dunes in the north and founded the city where the *Shalom Tower* stands today. They gave it the Hebrew name of Theodor Herzl's 'Old New Land' book: 'Spring Hill'. As early as 1887, some Jewish families left the Arab harbour town of Jaffa and founded a small settlement Neve Zedek outside its gates. This later became a residential area for artists, architects and well-off intellectuals in Tel Aviv after its foundation in 1909. Today, Neve Zedek is one of the most exclusive addresses in the city.

SIGHTSEEING

BAUHAUS ARCHITECTURE

In 2004, Unesco 'discovered' the city's Bauhaus architecture. Since then, a 'Bauhaus fever' broke out in Tel Aviv. Property owners and the city council are doing all they can to save at least 1000 (of around 4000) of the beautiful white houses built in the architectural style of the 1930s from going to ruin. Bauhaus exhibitions are being held in the city, window displays are dominated by Bauhaus designs, and an old, empty cinema has even been turned into a fascinating Bauhaus hotel. However, there is still a great deal that needs to be done. There are many dilapidated buildings standing alongside those that have been painstakingly renovated. The Bauhaus architecture is concentrated in the area around *Rothschild Boulevard* and *Dizengoff* and *Frishman Streets.* There is a new *Bauhaus Museum (Wed 11am–5pm, Fri 10am–2pm | Bialik St. 21 | free admission),* and the private *Bauhaus Center (Dizengoff St. 99 | tel. 03 5 22 02 49 | www.bauhaus-center.com)* organises guided tours (2 hours 15 US$ or 60 NIS).

BEN GURION HOUSE

The simple house where the founder of the State of Israel once lived. His library and many historical documents are on display here. *Sun, Tue–Thu 8am–3pm, Mon 8am–5pm, Fri 8am–1pm | Ben Gurion St. 17 | www.ben-gurion-house.org.il | free admission*

BETH HATEFUTSOT – DIASPORA MUSEUM

The 2000-year history of Jewish life in the Diaspora ('Dispersion') after 70AD is presented in a way that makes it easy to understand – this is a museum of the Jewish people in the real sense of the word. *Sun–Tue, Thu 10am–4pm, Wed 10am–6pm, Fri 9am–1pm | Ramat Aviv | University Complex (Gate 2, Klausner St.) | www.bh.org.il | entrance fee 35 NIS*

BIBLE MUSEUM

David Ben-Gurion proclaimed the independence of the State of Israel in the home of the first mayor of Tel Aviv Mir Dizengoff on 14 May, 1948. Today, it houses the *Bible Museum. Sun–Thu 9am–2pm | Rothschild Blvd. 16 | entrance fee 15 NIS*

FIRE AND WATER FOUNTAIN

Contemporary art in the centre of the city. The artist Yaacov Agam stacked five stainless steel rings of various sizes with coloured aluminium slats on top of each other to create cascades and fountains of water rising and falling in keeping with the rhythm of music. A flickering gas flame creates the illusion of a combination of fire and water while the fountain rotates. The fountain is a gift from Tel Aviv's twin town, Frankfurt am Main, in Germany. In summer, it rotates daily from 11am–1pm and again from 7pm–9pm – if it is not being repaired. It did not rotate at all for two years after 2009 because the upkeep had become too expensive for the city.

its bow document the history of immigration at the time of the British mandate. *Above the beach promenade, south of the Sheraton Hotel.*

HANAMAL – TEL AVIV PORT
Tel Aviv imitated the successful concept of other Mediterranean cities such as Genoa

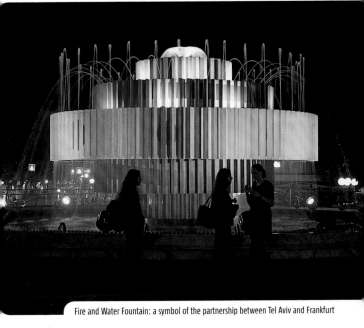

Fire and Water Fountain: a symbol of the partnership between Tel Aviv and Frankfurt

There were even plans to demolish the fountain but, in summer 2011, Yaacov Agam managed to get a court order stipulating that his 'artwork' be renovated. It started turning again in 2012. *Dizengoff Square*

HA APALAM MEMORIAL
In 2003, the Cohen family donated a monument to their father, the immigrant Michael Cohen. It has the structure of a ship and the impressive photographs on

and Barcelona by converting its former port into an exciting entertainment and shopping area. Tel Aviv Port, which is easy to reach on foot from the large beach hotels, is where young businesses experiment with new ideas in the former warehouses. Visitors will find restaurants with colourfully-painted façades, wide terraces and views of the sea. The cool breeze makes a stroll along the wooden planks of the passage a delightful experience – especially in the summer.

Old Yafo: taking a breather in front of St Peter's Church

mission to construct a railway line from Jaffa to Jerusalem. It started here at *Jaffa Train Station* that was opened in 1892. In 1900, the German Templer Hugo Wieland founded a brick and tile factory next to the tracks. The flourishing railway and building material business came to an abrupt end with the War of Independence in 1948. Starting half a century later, all 22 buildings in the complex were renovated, restored and once again made available to the public as a large cultural, shopping and recreational centre in 2010. Galleries, half a dozen restaurants and many art and design shops have breathed new life into the old station.

INSIDER TIP MUSEUM OF THE IZL (ETZEL MUSEUM)

The Museum of the Israeli Army documents the struggle of the Jewish underground movement Irgun Zvai Leumi (IZL) between 1947 and 1948 (the later Prime Minister Menachim Begin was an IZL officer) from a Zionist perspective. Immediately after the UN declaration made on 29 November, 1947 for a confederative, united Jewish-Arab state on the territory of the British mandate in Palestine, armed conflict (the so-called War of Independence) flared up. The aim in Tel Aviv was to take control of the then-Arab port of Jaffa. The museum that deals with these events in the first Middle East War was built as a dark cube of glass on the remnants of the walls of a house that was destroyed at the time. *Charles Clore Garden | directly on the beach on the shore promenade| Sun–Thu 8.30am–4pm | free admission).*

HATACHANA – THE STATION

Tel Aviv's historical railway station is not far from the beach in the south of the city. In 1888, the Ottoman Sultan gave the Jewish entrepreneur Yoseef Navon per-

OLD YAFO

Seen from the port, the backdrop of Yafo (Jaffa) looks like a fairy-tale city straight out of the Arabian Nights: walls staggered on top of and alongside each other, towers, rooftops and oriels form a district with picturesque small streets, artists' quarters, restaurants, shops and cafés.

The city is named after Japheth, Noah's youngest son. At the time of the crusades, it was turned into a fortress and called Joppa. After it had been completely destroyed by Napoleon in 1799, the Turks reconstructed the city. The city wall was torn down in 1906 and the stones used as construction material for the clock tower and other buildings. Old Yafo is a must for anyone visiting Israel. Small bazaars, galleries and studios, arts and crafts shops (open until late at night) and a flea market ensure that there is always something happening here in the narrow streets – which are, therefore, shady in summer. Every Wednesday at 9.30am tourists can take a free ● *Old Jaffa Tour* organised by the Tourist Information Office (2 hours, starting from the clock tower opposite the police station). *Tourist information: Old Jaffa Development Company | Mazal Degim St. 17 | tel. 03 5 18 40 15 | www.oldjaffa.co.il*

TEL AVIV MUSEUM OF ART

Impressive collection of international art and temporary exhibitions of works by Israeli artists. *Sat, Mon, Wed 10am–4pm, Tue, Thu 10am–10pm, Fri 10am–2pm | King Saul Blvd. 27 | www.tamuseum.com | entrance fee 15 NIS*

FOOD & DRINK

Two districts in Tel Aviv are ideal places to take a walk before you decide just which restaurant you want to visit.

You will probably think that there are at least as many restaurants as clothes shops on *Sheinkin Street* and their names are almost exclusively in Hebrew. Many are small bistro cafés with open-air terraces; most of them run by young people. The specialities are all rather similar but there are always fresh juices, snacks and burgers. And, there are also one or two 'better' restaurants in between the bistros. The large former warehouses in Tel Aviv's erstwhile port at the northern end of the

THE BEGINNING OF THE SABBATH

The Sabbath begins on Friday evening throughout Israel. Anybody staying in one of the better hotels – such as one of the Dans on Mount Carmel – should decide to have dinner in the largest restaurant in the hotel to be able to experience how pious Jews celebrate this holy day.

The restaurant tables are set especially beautifully; before sunset, the staff puts a bottle of wine and two candles on each table and there is always a splendid buffet. Religious Jews visit the synagogue in the hotel before coming to dinner. When the family is seated,

the male head begins with the *Kaddish*. He blesses a glass of wine with a sung prayer and then greets the Sabbath with a sip. After that, the *Challah* bread (a plaited loaf of bread sprinkled with poppy seeds and sesame) is blessed and given to all. Now the family shakes hands and heads for the buffet.

Every religious family celebrates this ceremony for itself. As not all of the hotel guests come to the restaurant at the same time, you will be able to experience this ritual several times in one evening. All the other families listen but don't let it disturb their meal.

beach near the city airport Dov, some 30 in number, have been converted into the entertainment district *TLV Port*. There are dozens of restaurants, most of them with terraces and a view of the Mediterranean. It's amazing what can be made out of a port. *All open daily at different times* | *Budget–Expensive*

INSIDER TIP **BOYA**

Inside: long, heavy wooden tables and damask; outside: elegant rattan chairs and sunshades. Interesting guests, young staff, excellent food. Frequent exhibitions. *Sun–Thu 9am–midnight, Sat 8am–midnight* | *Tel Aviv Port* | *tel. 03 5446166* | *www.boya.co.il* | *Moderate*

Dropping anchor – in the former port of Tel Aviv

ALADIN

Cosy little restaurant with a fabulous view of the skyline of Tel Aviv. *Daily* | *Mifratz Shlomo 5* | *tel. 03 6826766* | *Moderate*

BENEDIKT

Breakfast around the clock with everything the world's various cuisines have to offer; you should definitely try 'Eggs Benedict'. The restaurant has won several awards; young guests, courteous service. *Closed Fri/Sat* | *Ben Yehuda 171, corner of Jabotinsky Street* | *tel. 03 5440345* | *Budget*

INSIDER TIP **CAFÉ BATIA** ●

The oldest Jewish restaurant in the city (founded in 1941). Excellent East European food. Photos of famous guests on the walls. Kosher, of course. *Daily 11am–9pm* | *Dizengoff Street 197* | *tel. 03 5221335* | *Budget*

KING SALOMON

The restaurant in the Hilton Hotel is one of the most elegant – and most expensive – in Tel Aviv; heavily decorated, interesting guests. *Closed Fri/Sat* | *Independence Park* | *tel. 03 5202171* | *Expensive*

INSIDER TIP **MESSA**

The 'in' restaurant among the stylish establishments with first-class international cooking. On the ground floor of the *Millennium Tower* office building. Postmodern elegance with exquisite taste; long tables of light wood, the rest is black and white, City Line tableware and Philippe Starck WCs. *Daily | Ha Araba'a St. 19 | tel. 03 6 85 68 59 | www.messa.co.il | Expensive*

SHOPPING

Dizengoff and *Ben Yehuda* are the two main shopping streets with exquisite goods next to everyday articles and cheap things alongside the unaffordable. The 'in' crowd buy their clothes on *Sheinkin Street* and the most discriminating customers find what they are looking for on *Kikar ha Medina Square*.

Kerem Hateimanim ('The Yemenites' Vineyard') is the name of the area between Allenby Street and Hayarkon with the largest market in the city, the *Carmel Market*; bazaar-like atmosphere. *Mon–Sat 8am to around 6pm*

Not far away from Carmel Market, all of *Nachalat Binyamin Street* is turned into an *arts and crafts fair* where books, art and jewellery are sold twice a week *(Tue, Fri 10am–5pm)*. Artists also perform here. The historical Bauhaus district has a very special atmosphere. The *Bauhaus Center (Sun–Thu 10am–7.30pm, Fri 10am–2.30pm | Dizengoff St. 99)* sells beautiful designer articles.

'Mall shopping' is becoming increasingly popular in Israel; for example in the *Dizengoff Center (Dizengoff St., corner of King George St.)* or *Gan Ha'ir* in the *City Garden Mall (Ibn Givrol St. 71)*, both *Sun–Thu 9am–midnight, Fri 9am–4pm and 8pm–midnight.*

The largest selection of diamond jewellery can be found in the *Israel Diamond Center | Jabotinsky St. 1 | Ramat Gan | www.idc-diamond.com.*

CITY TOURS

The Tourist Information Centre offers four, free, guided walking tours dealing with specific aspects of Tel Aviv in English with expert guides.

GAY TEL AVIV

Its openness towards homosexuals has made Tel Aviv the gay capital of the Middle East. It celebrated its first Christopher Day Street Parade in 1998 and, in the same year, Israel's transsexual pop star Dana International won the Eurovision Song Contest.

Tel Aviv promotes itself throughout the world as a 'Gay Party capital'. The tourist information office publishes a 'Friends Gay Map' with information on hotels and the gay scene *(www.visitgay-tlv.com)*. Many private travel organisations offer weekend trips for international gays (for example, *www.gaytelaviv.net)* and those interested can buy the brochure published by the Israeli Embassy 'Homosexual Rights in Israel' *(www.israel.de)* at the airport in Tel Aviv. The hotels recommended by the scene provide their guests with a free English-Hebrew pocket dictionary with the title 'All you need to know to act and feel like a local'.

- *Every Sat 11am | meeting point: Rothschild Street 46, corner of Shadal St.* Subject: Bauhaus in Tel Aviv.
- *Every Wed, 9.30am | meeting point: clock tower, opposite the police station.* Subject: Old Jaffa (see p. 47).
- *Every Mon, 11am | meeting point: entrance to the university campus, Einstein Street/Syonon Bookshop.* Subject: the university, its history and significance.
- *Every Tue, 8pm | meeting point: Rothschild Street /Herzl Street* Subject: Tel Aviv by night (tour of the fashionable bars and restaurants).

BEACH

The ● *beach at Tel Aviv* is the most popular meeting place in the city. It is more than 50 yards wide and well cared for. Breakwaters off the coast mean that swimmers can bathe without danger. Light-coloured sand that is cleaned every morning, free public freshwater showers and a perfect infrastructure guarantee a wonderful day at the beach. Joggers get together here in the morning and evening and during the day the sand is the realm of sun-hungry beach fans. If you want to dive into the waves without being seen by members of the other sex, you can do it together with the city's orthodox citizens behind an impenetrable fence on *Metzitzim Beach* north of Independence Park.

ENTERTAINMENT

Tel Aviv Port is the newest entertainment district in the city. Here, you can stroll along the shore on the wooden boardwalk and visit chic restaurants, music cafés and discos.
The 'in' crowd gets together on *Sheinkin Street* in the evening – new shops, restaurants and cafés are opening all the time making sure that this street never loses any of its attraction. And, in summer, Friday is the night for beach parties!
Full details of evening entertainment can be found in the free monthly magazine 'Go Tel Aviv' (www.gotelaviv.co.il) available in hotels.

INSIDER TIP ▶ FREDERIC MANN AUDITORIUM ●

This is the home of the world famous *Israel Philharmonic Orchestra;* Zubin Mehta is its resident conductor. Concerts by international guest artists (mainly classical music) are also held here. *Hubermann Street 1, corner of Dizengoff St. | tel. 03 6 21 17 77 | www.ipo.co.il*

GALINA

Popular meeting place for young Israelis (DJ, mainstream music), dancing al-fresco on the terrace with a view of the sea or crowded inside. *Daily 7pm–3am | Tel Aviv Port | Hangar 19 | tel. 03 5 44 55 53 | free admission*

HA OMAN 17

One of the most popular clubs with international DJs. Thu, Fri and Sat enormous parties. *Daily from 9pm | Abarbanel Street 88 | entrance fee Sun–Wed 50 NIS, Thu–Sat 100 NIS*

SEA BREEZE SPA BAR

Restaurant, pub, bar and spa under a single roof. *Daily | Tel Aviv Port | Hangar 23 | tel. 03 5 44 42 14 | Moderate*

SHABUL JAZZ CLUB

The best live jazz in Israel. *Closed Sun | Live music from 10pm | Tel Aviv Port | Hangar 13*

WHERE TO STAY

Tel Aviv has the largest number of hotels in the country. If you want to stay on the beach, you should choose a hotel on Hayarkon Street. For an overview of hotels in Tel Aviv: *Tel Aviv Hotel Association | tel. 03 5 17 01 31 | www.telaviv.hotels.org.il. Dinami | tel. 03 7 41 47 95 | www.dinami.co.il* can provide holiday flats (min. stay: 3 days) in all parts of Tel Aviv.

CINEMA
Wonderful Bauhaus architecture: a 1930s cinema has been lavishly converted into a hotel with imaginative interior decoration. *82 rooms | Dizengoff Square | tel. 03 5 20 71 00 | www.atlas.co.il | Moderate*

DAN TEL AVIV
For years, this has been the 'in' hotel for VIPs visiting Tel Aviv. It is located directly on the beach, the large rooms have all the comfort expected in a hotel in this category. Elegant hotel, the only one in town with an indoor and outdoor pool. Perfect service. *286 rooms | Hayarkon St. 99 | tel. 03 5 20 25 25 | www.danhotels.com | Expensive*

INSIDER TIP ▶ HILTON TEL AVIV
The most traditional of the luxury hotels in Tel Aviv is located at the northern end of the beach. *583 rooms | Independence Park | tel. 03 5 20 22 22 | www.hilton.com | Expensive*

BNEI DAN YOUTH HOSTEL
Youth hostel in the northern part of the city on the Yarkon River (bus lines 4, 24, 45). *45 4- and 2-bed rooms | Bnei Dan St. 36 | tel. 03 5 44 17 48 | www.iyha.org.il | Budget*

INSIDER TIP ▶ NEVE TZEDEK
Intimate boutique hotel in the historical district of the same name (today it is one of the loveliest sections of Tel Aviv). The house is listed, the rooms are masterpieces of the interior decorator's art:

Cinema Hotel: most beautiful in 3D

many natural materials and lot of glass and greenery. *22 rooms | Dgania St. 4 | tel. 03 5 16 01 40 | www.nevetzedekhotel.com | Expensive*

SHERATON TEL AVIV HOTEL & TOWERS
One of the first skyscraper hotels on the beach in Tel Aviv. Spacious rooms, two swimming pools, perfect business centre. *313 rooms | Hayarkon St. 115 | tel. 03 5 21 11 11 | www.starwoodhotels.com | Expensive*

INFORMATION

TOURIST INFORMATION CENTER
Lahot Promenade, corner of Herbert Samuel St. *Tel. 03 5 16 61 88 | www.tel-aviv-gov.il.* And *www.telavivcity.com, www. telaviv-insider.co.il*
'Time out in Israel' with details of entertainment and cultural events is published every two months. *10 NIS; free, in hotels | digital.timeout.co.il*

WHERE TO GO

CAESAREA MARITIMA ★
(122 B5) (*ɯ D4*)
Caesarea (Hefar Qesari), 45km (28mi) north of Tel Aviv, is one of the most important excavation sites in Israel. The legendary Jewish uprising against the Romans which started in 66AD and led to the destruction of Israel in 70AD before finding a bloody end in 73AD on the rocky plateau of Masada, began in ancient Caesarea that had been built by Herod between 25 and 13BC. The excavations have still not been completed but the ruins of the forum, amphitheatre, hippodrome and Roman and Herodian aqueduct already give an impression of the former size and beauty of this city. To help your orientation: all the Roman ruins are in the *Caesarea National Park* north of the Sedat Yam (Sedot Yam) kibbutz. The aqueduct is 2km (1¼mi) away. *www.parks.org.il*
An elegant place to spend the night is INSIDER **TIP** *Dan Caesarea*, Israel's only hotel with its own golf course – 18 holes in front of the door *(114 rooms | tel. 06 6 26 9111 | www.danhotels.com | Expensive)*. A stylish but not overly expensive restaurant near the Roman ruins is also the clubhouse *(Nineteen Caesarea | tel. 04 6 26 70 00 | daily 9am–10pm | Moderate)*. Lovely terrace with a view of the greens and fairways.

BOOKS & FILMS

▶ **Once upon a Country: A Palestinian Life** – Sari Nusseibeh describes the similarities that exist between people of different faiths in the Holy Land with humour and wisdom and how insanity makes itself felt in Jerusalem

▶ **Detail** (2004) – This short documentary film by the Israeli director Avi Mograbi showing the difficulties the Israeli army has dealing with Palestinian civilians has been awarded many prizes

▶ **The Heart of Jenin** (2008) – The Palestinian Ismail Khatib donated the organs of his son who had been killed by Israeli soldiers to Israeli children.

The German-American team of directors Marcus Vetter and Leon Geller focus on the father and the reasons for his decision

▶ **Waltz with Bashir** – Ari Folman reflects on the nightmares he faced after his deployment as a soldier in the Lebanon War. The animated film received international acclaim after it was awarded the Golden Globe and César in 2009

▶ **Exodus** – Otto Preminger filmed Leon Uris' bestseller about the fate of Jewish emigrants on the ship 'Exodus' with Paul Newman in the lead role in 1960

Caesarea Maritima: bathing with the crusaders

HERZLIYA (122 A6) (*Ø D5*)

This town on the Mediterranean coast with a population of 75,000 was founded in 1924 and named after Theodor Herzl. Herzliya (Herzliyya) has a beautiful long sandy beach and the hotels in all price categories show just how important it is as a seaside resort. With its ideal location on the beach, *Dan Accadia (207 rooms | tel. 09 9 59 70 70 | www.danhotels.com | Expensive)* offers its guests comfort and tranquillity.

NETANYA (122 B5) (*Ø D5*)

This seaside resort owes its existence to the citrus fruit that is grown in the area which needed a transport centre. The beautiful sandy beach soon attracted Israeli and foreign tourists and the town developed into a popular holiday destination. Today, Netanya (pop. 150,000) – approx. 30km (18mi) north of Tel Aviv – is Israel's largest seaside resort with large and small hotels in all price categories and organised entertainment to suit all tastes.

In addition, Netanya has now developed into the centre of the Israeli diamond industry. Many small and large enterprises create dazzling diamonds out of imported raw stones. Most are exported but there are still many jewellery shops including *Diamimon (Gad Mahnas St. 2)*. *Tourist information: Kikar Hatzmaut | tel. 09 8 82 72 86 | www.netanya.muni.il*

If you are looking for a peaceful beach, historically important *Apollonia* with its beautiful lagoon is in the immediate vicinity.

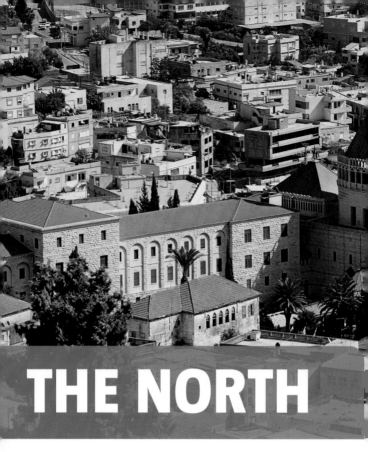

THE NORTH

Birds are careful about where they choose to spend the winter. The climate, the air, the vegetation, everything must be just right. That means that there must be good reasons for hundred of species of migratory birds settling in northern Israel between September and April every year.

Here – especially in Upper Galilee – it is peaceful; the countryside is still unspoilt and relatively sparsely populated and there are also large protected nature reserves. The north of Israel, between the Yezreel Plain and Lebanese border, biblical Galilee with Nazareth, Tiberias and the Sea of Galilee, the region where Jesus spent the major portion of His life.

The mountains of Galilee rise up to 1200m (4000ft) in the north in Har Meron; in the east, the Golan Heights, occupied by Israel, border on the Jordan Valley and the fertile Hule Plain. If you follow the Jordan to the south, you reach the Sea of Galilee, one of the places where Jesus was which is today the tourist centre of the entire region with all kinds of sports, bathing and spa complexes. Away from the major centres, the north of Israel offers possibilities to relax in natural surroundings. This region was also on the route of the old caravan trails between Asia, Africa and Europe meaning that there are important archaeological sites waiting to be explored:

Photo: View over Nazareth

The land of Jesus – most of the biblical places lie in agrarian Galilee in the north of Israel

ruined Canaanite cities, Roman temples, mountain fortresses from the age of the Islamic and Crusade periods, synagogues from the age of the Talmud and mediaeval mysticism.

NAZARETH

(122 C3–4) (*ɯ E4*) **Nazareth (Nazerat; pop. 65,000) has been inhabited since biblical days and gained its importance through Jesus.**

This is where He spent His young years, where He developed His religious concepts and began teaching. That is why there are many churches in Nazareth named after events in Jesus' life. Today, Nazareth is still located in the midst of fields, orchards and vineyards as if time had stood still. But, large new zones of Jewish settlements have been

The largest Christian building in the Middle East: the Basilica of the Annunciation in Nazareth

built on the slopes of Nazareth that have now merged to form Nazareth-Ilit.

After Sultan Beibars drove the crusaders out of the city in 1263, no Christians were allowed to live in it until well into the 17th century. (The Hebrew word for Christians 'Natzri' comes from Natzrat, the Hebrew name of Nazareth.) Today, Nazareth is the largest Arab city in Israel where around 35% of the population are Palestinian Christians. They live there without any conflicts with the Palestinian Moslems. All of the biblical sites are in the centre of the city and easy to reach on foot.

SIGHTSEEING

INSIDER TIP ST GABRIEL CHURCH

Earlier tradition believed that the Archangel Gabriel appeared before the Virgin Mary here and not in the Church of the Annunciation. Until 1263, this was the site of a Crusaders' church built over a spring whose water flows into nearby Mary's Well. The Greek Orthodox St Gabriel Church with its magnificent iconostasis has stood on exactly the same spot since 1750. Traces of the crusaders can still be seen in the grotto. The church is a place of profound silence. *Daily 8am–6pm | Al Chanuk Rd. | free admission*

ST JOSEPH CHURCH

In 1911, a decision was made to erect a church where Joseph's workshop once stood on foundations from the age of the crusades only a few yards north of the Church of the Annunciation. There is a grotto underneath the church where the Holy Family is said to have lived at one time. *Daily 7am–5pm (in summer 6pm) | Baborat Rd. | free admission*

SYNAGOGUE CHURCH

There is a Greek Catholic church on the site behind the main market where the Jew Jesus (Luke 4:16) visited the synagogue on the Sabbath, read the Torah before the congregation and declared himself the one who would fulfil the prophesies of Isaiah (Isaiah 61). The church, built by the crusaders, was in the possession of Roman Catholic Franciscan monks before the Turkish Sultan Daher El Omar gave it to the Greek Orthodox Melkites in 1741. *Mon–Sat 8am–6pm, Sun 8am–11.30am | free admission*

BASILICA OF THE ANNUNCIATION ●

The most important attraction in Nazareth and, at the same time, one of the largest Christian churches in the Middle East, has stood precisely on the site where the major Christian religions believe that the Archangel Gabriel told the Virgin Mary that she was to give birth to Jesus *(Casa Nova St)* since 1966. Architecturally, the Renaissance Revival building is divided into two sections: the upper part is devoted to the Virgin Mary and her cult while the Grotto of the Annunciation and the ruins of a crusaders' basilica have been integrated into the lower part. The church's tower is 47m (154ft) high. *Mon–Sat 8am–noon and 2pm–6pm (in winter 5pm) | free admission*

FOOD & DRINK

LA FONTANA DI MARIA

Stylish restaurant with Arab-Oriental cuisine. Its closeness to 'Mary's Well', from where it is said that Mary used to draw her water and which is still intact, inspired the decoration of the walls. Especially tasty: the Joseph kebab. *Daily | Hama'ayan Square | tel. 04 6 46 04 35 | Moderate*

HOLYLAND INN

Opposite the Church of the Annunciation, attuned to the taste of groups of western visitors. Large selection of Oriental and international dishes. *Daily | Paul VI St. | tel. 04 6 57 54 15 | Budget*

SHOPPING

Apart from in Jerusalem, nowhere else in Israel will you find such an conglomeration of shops selling religious articles as in the centre of Nazareth. Tourists will also find the bazaar interesting; it is a little off the beaten track at the end of *Casa Nova St.*

WHERE TO STAY

CASA NOVA

Christian hostel opposite the Church of the Annunciation; not only for pilgrims. Simply furnished rooms. If you don't want to be wakened in the morning by the singing of pilgrims on their way to the Church of the Annunciation, ask for a room in the rear courtyard. *62 rooms | Casa Nova St. | tel. 04 6 57 13 67 | Moderate*

AL MUTRAN GUESTHOUSE

The 200-year-old house of the Qattouf family of Arab jeweller's has been transformed into a very delightful guesthouse in the centre of town not far away from the holy sites. North of the Church of the Annunciation, near St Gabriel Church. *4 suites with 3 or 4 rooms | Paul VI St. | tel. 04 6 45 79 47 | www.al-mutran.com | Moderate*

MARCO POLO HIGHLIGHTS

★ **Belvoir**
The ruins of a crusaders' fortress from the 12th century has magnificent views → p. 60

★ **Hazor**
This was the most powerful city in Canaan in biblical times and is now the perfect place to stay and learn about everyday life on a kibbutz → p. 62

Marriage church in Canaan: waiting for the miracle of the wine?

PLAZA HOTEL ☆☆

8-storey hotel monster above the Old Town, standardised luxury, swimming pool. Beautiful view of Nazareth, but comfort has its price: it is a long way from the main Christian sites. *184 rooms. | Hermon Street 2 | tel. 04 6 02 82 00 | www.plaza-nazarethilit.co.il | Expensive*

INFORMATION

NAZARETH CULTURE AND TOURISM ASSOCIATION

In Khan El Basha Building | Casa Nova St. | tel. 04 6 01 10 72 | www.nazarethinfo.org

WHERE TO GO

INSIDERTIP KANA (CANA)
(122 C3) (⍥ E3)

Jesus turned water into wine (John 2:1–11) – a miracle one would like to see happen more often – at the wedding in Kana (Kafr Kanna), the birthplace of Bartholomew the Apostle, 10km (6mi) northeast of Nazareth. Since 1881, this has been the site of a Franciscan church in which old wine amphorae and a section of mosaic floor from the early Middle Ages recall the event. The walls of the church are decorated with extremely colourful paintings showing the miracle of the transformation. *(Mon–Fri 9am–noon and 2pm–5pm, Sat 9–noon).*

TABOR ☆☆ (122 C4) (⍥ E4)

Biblical Mount Tabor (Tavor), which later became a Christian episcopal see, lies some 10km (6mi) east of Nazareth; it is considered to be the site of the 'Transfiguration of Jesus'. The Franciscans have had a large monastery complex here, in which an early-Christian church and crusaders' basilica are integrated, since 1631.

TIBERIAS

(123 D3) (⍥ E3) **Tiberias (Teverya; pop. 50,000) is the most important city on the Sea of Galilee. Today – as in Roman times – it is a popular holiday destination with spa facilities.**

The curative and prophylactic qualities of its thermal springs, the subtropical climate (in summer up to 35°C (95°F) and around 21°C (70°F) in winter) and the high atmospheric pressure (the city is 200m/650ft below sea level) guarantee that its visitors feel good. The large hotels and city centre lie directly on the shore of the lake; behind it, to the west, Tiberias is expanding up the wooded slopes of the Galilean mountains. The ☆ hotels built there have magnificent views of the lake.

This city was founded by Herod Antipas in 18AD in honour of the Roman emperor and named after him – the splendour and beauty of ancient Hamat Tiberias was described by Flavius Josephus. In the 3rd century, it developed into a centre of Jewish scholarship. Tiberias' economic power even made it possible for it to survive during the wars between the crusaders and Moslems. In April 1948, Israeli troops conquered Tiberias and now only a handful of Palestinians live here.

SIGHTSEEING

OLD TOWN
Old Tiberias lies directly on the lake; it was once surrounded by an almost 1500m (5000ft)-long wall. The ruins, citadel and old street still bear witness to the urban culture that characterised Tiberias in the age of the crusaders and while the city was under Arab rule in the 17th and 18th centuries. The remains from the Roman period and the hot springs, which were already famous in Antiquity and are considered to be the oldest on earth, are 8km (5mi) to the south in *Hamat Tiberias*.

TOMB OF RABBI AKIVA ☆
Memorial to the rabbi who was skinned alive by the Romans during the Bar Kochba Revolt in 135. The tomb, with its white dome, is very popular with tourists because there is a wonderful view far over the Sea of Galilee, the city of Tiberias and the Golan Heights from it. *Entrance only from Trumpeldor St.*

HAMAM SULEIMAN MUSEUM
Museum on the cultural history of the baths and spa in *Hamat Tiberias National Park. Sat–Thu 8am–5pm (Oct–March 4pm), Fri 8am–noon | entrance fee 15 NIS*

FOOD & DRINK

DECKS
It is very loud in this grill restaurant that juts out into the lake at the end of the promenade along the shore but this is made up for by the excellent fish served. *Daily | Lido Beach | tel. 04 6 72 15 38 | Moderate*

GALEI GIL
Expertly prepared John Dory is served at tables set with white linen in this fish restaurant on the lake. *Daily | Beach Promenade | tel. 04 6 72 06 99 | Moderate*

SPORTS & ACTIVITIES

SAILING AND SURFING
The *Kinnereth Sailing Company* on the shore promenade organises boat trips and rents rowing and sailing boats, as well as surfboards, to watersports fans. One of the main attractions is a trip across the lake in the 'Jesus Boat' – a copy of a wooden boat from the 1st century. *Tel. 04 6 72 30 06*

ENTERTAINMENT

The ☆ ● *Tayyelet*, a lovely promenade, runs along the shore of the lake and is especially attractive for an evening stroll. The view is breathtaking: you can see across to the illuminated settlements on the eastern shore of the lake and up to the Golan Heights. There is an aluminium sculpture showing the contours of the lake and the actual water level at the end of the promenade.

WHERE TO STAY

INSIDER TIP ▶ **KAREI DESHE YOUTH HOSTEL**

The most beautiful youth hostel in Israel is located 12km (7½mi) to the north of Tiberias directly on the lake. Part of the complex has been expanded to include a top category guesthouse. There is no better place on the lake for those looking for seclusion. *80 beds (also single and double rooms) | tel. 04 6 72 06 01 | kdeshe@iyha.org.il | Budget*

TABGHA PILGRIMS' HOUSE

The Catholic *Deutscher Verein vom heiligen Land* has operated a very pleasant guesthouse for pilgrims since 1889. It has a large garden in an absolutely peaceful location on the northern shore of the Sea of Galilee. *68 rooms| Habanim St. | tel. 04 6 70 01 00 | pilgerhaus@tabgha.org.il | Moderate*

INSIDER TIP ▶ **THE SCOTS HOTEL** ☼ ☺

The Scottish Church has transformed its historical hospital in the centre above the lake into a very impressive hotel. The food is prepared using spices and herbs from its own garden. Wine cellar in the vaults, art gallery and swimming pool. The best hotel in Tiberias – and one with an exciting history. *65 rooms | tel. 04 6 71 07 10 | www.scotshotels.co.il | Expensive*

INFORMATION

TOURIST INFORMATION GO GALILEE
Jordan Street 1 | tel. 06 6 79 19 81 | www.tiberias.muni.il

WHERE TO GO

BELVOIR ★ ☼ (123 D4) (⌂ E4)
A long, steep, narrow road that branches off Highway 90 towards the west leads up to this beautiful old crusaders' fortress 16km (10mi) to the south of the lake. The fortress was built in 1140 and belonged to the Knights Hospitaller until it was conquered by Sultan Saladin in 1189. The massive ruins still give an impression of the strategic significance of the castle.

LOW BUDGET

▶ Young people who want to find out what life on a kibbutz is really like can satisfy their curiosity and get free board and lodging if they are prepared to do agricultural work for 6 hours a day for at least one week at the *Ayelet Hashahar* kibbutz north of the Sea of Galilee not far from Rosh Pina. Volunteers working at Ayelet Hashahar can also visit the archaeological site at Hazor free of charge. *Advanced registration necessary | www.ayelet.org.il or via the National Council of Volunteering | www.ivolunteer.org.il*

▶ Everything revolves around the Virgin Mary, Joseph and their Son in the 'Most Christian' town in Galilee, in Nazareth. The well in a cave a few yards to the north of the Church of the Annunciation bears Mary's name. Elias and Marina Shama opened their *Cactus* souvenir shop right next to *Mary's Well*; there is also an old bathhouse beneath it. You can buy inexpensive religious articles in the shop and also visit the Roman baths free of charge *(www.nazarethbathhouse.com)*.

Only a small part of the ancient city complex: the Roman theatre in Bet Shean

Magnificent views over the Jordan Valley. *Sat–Thu 8am–5pm, Fri 8am–2pm | entrance fee 23 NIS*

INSIDER TIP **THE MOUNT OF BEATITUDES** ⚘ (123 D3) (*M E3*)
Jesus summarised the core message of his teachings and said the Lord's Prayer for the first time in the Sermon on the Mount of Beatitudes on the northwest shore of the Sea of Galilee (Matthew 5–7). The mountain with the *Church of the Beatitudes (daily 8am–noon and 2.30–5pm)* is 4km (2½mi) away from *Tabgha*. After the ascent, you will be rewarded with a wonderful panoramic view. Tip: you will be following in Jesus' footsteps if you hike up to the Mount of Beatitudes from Tabgha *(www.biblewalks.com)*.

BET SHEAN (123 D4) (*M E4*)
In ancient times, the city of Bet Shean (Bet She'an, 24km/15mi south of the Sea of Galilee) was one of the most important trading centres in Palestine. The impressive *Roman theatre*, one of the most beautiful Roman buildings in the entire country, is especially interesting; it had seating for as many as 7000 spectators. The large *spa complex* the *Nymphaeum* is another archaeological highlight, as are the magnificent long colonnades on *Palladius Street*. *Oct–March daily 8am–4pm, Nov–April Sun–Thu 8am–8pm, Fri/Sat 8pm–5pm | entrance fee 35 NIS*

EN GEV ● (123 D3) (*M F3*)
The most convenient way to reach the kibbutz 8km (5mi) to the east is by taking a steamer across the lake – by road it is a 23km (14mi) drive along the southern shore. It has a leisure centre, camping area, the *Esco Music Center* where the 'En Gev Music Festival' is held every year, as well as a ⚘ restaurant on the shore of the lake. There is a wonderful view over

the Sea of Galilee to Tiberias from the kibbutz' own fish restaurant. The kibbutz also runs a hotel, the *Holiday Resort (88 rooms, 63 chalets | tel. 04 6 65 98 00 | www.eingev.org.il | Moderate)* 2km (1¼mi) to the south.

INSIDER TIP GINOSSAR
(123 D3) (*ⁿⁿ E3*)

Ginossar (Ginnosar) is a kibbutz on the north-western shore of the lake with an important archaeological find. In 1986, a year of drought when the water level of the lake was very low, two fishermen discovered a 2000-year-old wooden boat in the sediment.

GOLAN HEIGHTS
(123 D–E 1–3) (*ⁿⁿ F2–3*)

The Golan Heights are an approximately 69km (43mi)-long and 26 (16mi)-wide range of hills in Syria from where the Syrians fired at Israeli villages after 1948. In 1967, Israel occupied a large section of the area and later settled it until finally declaring it annexed to Israel in 1980. Arab Druzes live on the Golan. There is a splendid view over the entire Sea of Galilee from the *Peace Observation Point* in *Kefar Haruv*.

HAZOR ★
(123 D2) (*ⁿⁿ E3*)

Hazor, which was the most powerful city in Canaan, is located 15km (9mi) north of the Sea of Galilee next to the *Ayelet Hashahar Kibbutz* founded in 1919. Today, it is one of the largest excavation sites. The palaces, temples, walls and fortifications from the age of King Solomon – 10th century BC – are especially fascinating. There is a model of the massive complex of old Hazor in the *Kibbutz Museum (April– Sept Sat–Thu 8am–5pm, Fri 8am–2pm, Oct–March Sat–Thu 8am–4pm | entrance fee10 NIS)*. The kibbutz also runs a com-

fortable guesthouse *(22 rooms | tel. 04 6 73 39 99 | Moderate)*.

CAPERNAUM
(123 D3) (*ⁿⁿ E3*)

The New Testament (Matthew 9:1) tells that the small harbour village of *Kefar Nahum* on the north shore of the Sea of Galilee was one of the places where Jesus liked to preach. This is also where he met Peter, one of his disciples. The Roman excavations, a synagogue from the 4th century, as well as the octagonal *Peter's House (daily 8.30am–4pm | entrance fee 10 NIS)* that was built in the 5th century, are all important sites. There is a ferry between Tiberias and Capernaum *(only July, Aug: travel time 45 mins.)*.

SAFED
(123 D2) (*ⁿⁿ E3*)

Zefat, the city of the Cabbalists with its many synagogues, is one of the four holy cities in Israel. It achieved historical importance when the crusaders killed all of the Jews in Safed in a pogrom. The city is located 24km (15mi) north of Tiberias at an altitude of almost 900m (3000ft) on a mountain where there are also the ruins of a fortress, originally built by the Romans and subsequently expanded by the crusaders, the Mamalukes and finally by the Turks. The old Jewish district is on the south side of the mountain slope. Some of the houses date from the 16th century, the time of the mystical Torah interpretations *(kabala)* made by the local rabbis who turned Safed into a new religious centre. Today, around 30,000 people live in the town. Wandering through the narrow streets, visitors feel the fascinating mixture of a religious stronghold (more than ten synagogues, many private Jewish schools) and a carefree worldly lifestyle (pedestrian precincts with pavement cafés, galleries and boutiques).

Pleasantly unassuming architecture: the Church of the Multiplication in Tabgha

SEA OF GALILEE (123 D3) (*m E–F 3–4*)

The Sea of Galilee is Israel's largest freshwater lake and, as such, one of the country's major natural resources. A pipeline supplies many cities and even the Negev desert with water from the lake. The Sea of Galilee is some 11km (7mi) from east to west and about 21km (13mi) from north to south; it is up to 50m (165ft) deep, lies 200m (650ft) below sea level and the Jordan River flows through it. Its Hebrew name *Yam Kinnereth* (*kinner* = harp) was given to it by the Lord himself: it is said that he compared the sound of its waves with that of a harp. The lake played a major role in Jesus' life as told in the New Testament. Many of His activities and miracles took place at the lake itself or places in the immediate vicinity.

In most of the areas where there are no buildings or kibbutzim, the lake shore is rather stony. The eastern sections are more deserted and some attractive small sandy beaches can be found in the northeastern corners. It is possible to hire windsurfing boards in the holiday resort Ma'agan operated by the kibbutz of the same name on the south shore of the Sea of Galilee (*Ma'agan Holiday Village | at the southern tip of the Sea of Galilee | tel. 04 6 65 44 33 | www.maagan.com | 1 hour 30 NIS*).

INSIDER TIP ▶ TABGHA (123 D3) (*m E3*)

One of the most famous miracles in the Bible took place on the northern shore of the Sea of Galilee. Before holding the Sermon on the Mount of Beatitudes, Jesus fed the multitude of 5000 people with the day's ration of one of the fishermen. This miracle is recalled in the *Church of the Multiplication (daily 8.30–5pm)*. It was erected on the foundations of the original church from the 5th century and has a mosaic floor that is well worth seeing. A path leads from the church grounds through a beautiful garden to the lake. This site is particularly popular among pilgrims as a place to visit and pray. Tabgha is 11km (7mi) north of Tiberias.

JERUSALEM

CITY WHERE TO START?
Jaffa Gate (U C4) (📍 c4): most of the important sights are located within the walls of the Old City of Jerusalem and it is easy to walk to many of them from Jaffa Gate. Taxis and buses depart from here for West Jerusalem – e.g. to the *Knesset* and *Yad Vashem (lines 9, 17, 24 | fare 5 NIS | not on the Sabbath)*. You should avoid driving to Jerusalem in a hired car; the street signs are only in Hebrew and there are very few, very expensive, parking spaces.

MAP INSIDE BACK COVER
The city of Jerusalem (Yerushalayim) (125 D2) (📍 E6–7) lies 800m (2600ft) above sea level in the mountains of Judea, some 69km (43mi) east of Tel Aviv. The border of the Kingdom of Jordan ran immediately in front of the city wall until 1967; approx. 800,000 people live within the city limits of Jerusalem unilaterally expanded by Israel.

In the Middle Ages, pilgrims needed more than a week to travel from the coast 'up to Jerusalem'. In 1898, it still took the German Emperor two days for the tour when he travelled to Ottoman Jerusalem for the first time for the consecration of

Photo: Jerusalem, view of the Dome of the Rock

Yerushaliyim and El Kuds – for Israelis, Jerusalem is the 'Place of Peace', for Arabs 'The Holy'

the Protestant Church of the Redeemer. Today, this is only a 40-minute drive on Highway No. 1. This makes Jerusalem an ideal starting point for travelling around the country.

Nowhere else do the three monotheistic religions come as close to each other as they do in Jerusalem. For the Jews, this is where King Solomon built the Great Temple; for the Christians, the city is closely linked to the work, death and resurrection of Jesus; for Moslems, the Dome of the Rock and Al Aqsa Mosque are two of the holiest sites. These places of religious veneration that attract hundreds of thousands of pilgrims every year lie in the immediate vicinity of each other in the Old City.

Just as at the time of the biblical apostles, the best way to get around inside the walled Old City is on foot. Visitors enter the maze of streets through one of the seven massive gates (the eighth, the Golden Gate, has been bricked up for centuries) and, at first, might have difficulty finding their way. However, small street signs make it a simple matter to

and, until today, both Israelis and Palestinians still claim possession of that section of Jerusalem that was not part of Israel before 1967. Jerusalem has been rebuilt no matter how often it was destroyed – and, since 1967, more beautifully than ever before.

The fragrance of the Orient: food souk in the Old Town of Jerusalem

get to the main attractions without a map. Allow plenty of time for the Old City, wander through the bazaars, drink a cup of coffee with cardamom or peppermint tea in an Arab or Armenian café, and relax for a while, before rushing off to the next highlight or throwing yourself into the adventure of bargaining and buying. *Yerushalayim* , the Hebrew name of the city, means 'Place of Peace'. In Arabic, it is called *El Kuds* 'The Holy'. However, war and not peace seems to be more characteristic of Jerusalem; the city has suffered armed combat 36 times in its history; it was destroyed more than a dozen times

After the end of the Six Day War in 1967, Israel occupied the eastern section of Jerusalem including the Old City and proclaimed it the capital of the state. The United Nations did not recognise this action. On 30 July, 1980, the Knesset confirmed the annexation: 'Jerusalem, complete and united, is the capital of Israel'. Jerusalem, the divided city, now reunited? This creates a false impression because it immediately gives rise to comparisons with other divided cities such as Berlin. However, Jerusalem was never divided in such a way. After the 1949 armistice, the dividing line did not run through a city with the deep-rooted traditions of a homogeneous population but between the new city erected in the west by Israel with its almost exclusively Jewish inhabitants and the section in the east – including the Old City, historical Jerusalem – that, with the exception of a small Jewish quarter, was solely the home of Arabs.

The Knesset proclamation in 1980 intensified the positions and, in addition, Ariel Sharon (a later Prime Minister) demonstratively moved into a house in the Arab section near Damascus Gate claiming that, at the time of the Ottoman Empire, this had belonged to one of his Jewish forefathers. It is a matter of course that Palestinians react to this kind of provocation with civil violence that then provokes reciprocal violence from the State of Israel.

Teddy Kollek, who had migrated from Austria, held the office of Mayor of Jerusalem from 1965 to 1993. He always argued that peace and peaceful coexistence were not merely a goal but also a means for achieving peace. That is why he opposed the missionary zeal of the fanatics who wanted to extend their lifestyle out of their district of Mea Shearim to all of Jerusalem (including using force to impose a ban on driving on the Sabbath) and against the provocation of the fanatic Gush Emunim settlers who hold Jewish prayer services between the Dome of the Rock and Al Aqsa Mosque.

His successors from the conservative Likud, Ehud Olmert (1994–2003 and Prime Minister until 2009) and Uri Lupolianski (2003–08) did not think very much of 'peaceful coexistence' and promoted the notion of 'a complete and united capital' by erecting new Jewish settlements in the Arab east section of Jerusalem. Since then, the 'Israelisation' of East Jerusalem has been accompanied by suicide attacks and the construction of a wall on Palestinian territory. The secular, right-wing nationalist Nir Birkat has been Mayor of Jerusalem since 2009. In 2010, he permitted a Jewish prayer school to occupy the third floor and roof of a Palestinian house opposite the fifth station on the Via Dolorosa and hang

MARCO POLO HIGHLIGHTS

half a dozen gigantic Israeli flags in the centre of the Arab quarter (easy to see from the Austrian Hospice). Since 1967, Jerusalem's Palestinians have boycotted the parliamentary elections of the 'occupational force, Israel'.

After 1967, Israel unilaterally expanded the borders of the city and extended the urban area of Jerusalem to the east. The city is now surrounded by a ring of Jewish housing estates and today there are as many Jewish Israelis as Palestinians in occupied East Jerusalem. In 2004, Israel started building a 8m (25ft)-high concrete wall with watchtowers through the centre of Palestinian villages and, in this way, completely isolated Palestinian East Jerusalem from the West Bank. The United Nations protested but they are powerless against the construction of the wall that the Israelis call an 'anti-terror fence'.

Jerusalem – three religions, two peoples, one city! For the Palestinians and the entire Arab world, Jerusalem is part of the package of any peace negotiations. As everybody is aware of the great symbolic significance Jerusalem has for Jews, it is necessary to find a compromise. Jerusalem must remain one city but, because two peoples live there, it can also be the 'capital' of two states – Israel and Palestine – with independent communal administrations under the auspices of an overall communal council. The Israeli writer and former representative in the Knesset Uri Avnery and the Palestinian journalist Hanna Siniora have been promoting this solution, which the UN had already foreseen with the 'internationalisation' of Jerusalem in 1947, for many years.

The 122nd Psalm says: 'Pray for the peace of Jerusalem: they shall prosper that love thee. Peace be within thy walls, and prosperity within thy palaces. For my brethren and companions' sakes, I will now say, Peace be within thee.' Today, the sentiments of the psalmist are much more relevant than ever before.

SIGHTSEEING

AL AQSA MOSQUE AND THE DOME OF THE ROCK ★
(U D–E 3–4) (*m d–e 3–4*)

The Dome of the Rock with its golden cupola and the Al Aqsa mosque on the Temple Mount are two of the major sights in Jerusalem; both are under Moslem Awqaf administration but access is controlled by Israel. There are restricted possibilities to visit the Temple Mount; in exceptional cases, groups can be admitted to the mosques if arrangements are made in advance (tel. 03 6 22 62 50).

No other building is a more powerful symbol of the connections that exist between Judaism, Christianity and Islam than the Dome of the Rock (Qubbet es-Sakhra). Its golden cupola, with a diameter of 26m (85ft), arches over where a Jewish temple used to stand where Abraham was to sacrifice Isaac, and also the rock from where the Prophet Mohammed rode into heaven on his horse Al Burak. The 16 beautiful coloured windows in the tambour of this octagonal mosque, which Caliph Malik Ibn Marwa had erected in the year 691, are among the most precious artworks in Islam.

The Al Aqsa Mosque, next to the Dome of the Rock, in the southern section of the Temple Mount is the largest mosque in Jerusalem – inside, 5000 faithful can bow towards Mecca at any one time. It was erected by Caliph Abdul Walid, the son of the man who built the Dome of the Rock, in 714 and marks the end point of Mohammed's miraculous journey from Mecca to, what was at the time, the most distant mosque in Jerusalem (in Arabic,

'Al Aqsa' means the furthest). Caliph Al-Sahir renovated the mosque in 1034 following an earthquake and donated the dazzling dome.

For more than 1300 years, the Dome of the Rock and Al Aqsa Mosque, the third most holy site for all Moslems after Mecca and Medina, have stood on the massive plateau the Israelis call the *Temple Mount (Mount Moriah)*, as it was the site of the First and Second Temples. The Temple Mount is surrounded by walls – including the so-called Western or Wailing Wall. Jews are not allowed to set foot on the Temple Mount because – in the position taken by the High Rabbinate – they could accidently walk on the spot that, in biblical times, could only be touched by the High Priest. But, not all Jewish Israelis pay attention to that: in order to underline Jewish claims to the Temple Mount, some of them provocatively celebrated their prayers between the two mosques and have attempted to lay a foundation stone for the Third Temple on several occasions. Tourist are only able to go up to the Temple Mount along a wooden bridge (next to the Western Wall) and are subjected to extremely rigorous Israeli security controls *Sun–Thu 7.30am–11am and 12.30pm–2.30pm | free admission*. Currently, it is not possible for individual tourists to visit the two mosques.

ST ANNE'S CHURCH (U E3) (*Ⓜ e3*)

In their zeal to bring Palestine completely under Christian influence, the crusaders built churches wherever they could as a sign of their claim to power. St Anne's Church, in honour of the Mother of Mary, was built for this purpose in the 12th century. It is next to *St Stephen's Gate* and is one of the best-preserved crusaders' buildings in Palestine. The *Pool of Bethesda* is next to it. *Mon–Sat 8am–5pm (April–Sept 6pm) | admission free*

Jerusalem's most magnificent building – the Dome of the Rock

(U C4–5) (🗺 c4–5)

This is a pleasantly relaxed district in Jerusalem's Old City with a mixture of residential buildings, churches, libraries and monasteries – no shops, no cafés and no restaurants to take your mind off things. The Armenian community and its patriarch, the religious leader in Israel, have lived here for almost 2000 years. The focal point of the quarter is *St James' Cathedral* built in the 12th century and named after one of Jesus' disciples *(daily 3pm–3.45pm, Mon–Fri 6.30am–7.30am, Sat 6.30am–9.30am)*. The *Museum for Armenian History (Mon–Sat 10am–4.30 pm | admission free)* is also well worth visiting.

MOUNT ZION (U C5) (🗺 c5)

King David's Tomb is located on a little hill to the southwest of the city walls near Zion Gate *(Sun–Thu 8am–5pm, Fri 8am–1pm)*. Jesus and his disciples celebrated the Last Supper in the rooms opposite this *(Cenaculum, Room of the Last Supper | daily 8am–5pm)*. Catholics worship the place where Mary died and ascended into heaven in the neighbouring church *(Dormition Abbey | Mon–Fri 8.30am–noon and 12.30–5.30pm)* which was built by German Benedictines between 1903 and 1910. According to the Bible, Jesus was rejected three times by his disciple Peter 'before the cock crowed'. The faithful recall this in the chapel of *St Peter in Gallicantu (daily 8.30am–5pm)*.

Today, *The Chamber of the Holocaust*, next to King David's Tomb serves as a memorial to the Jewish victims of National Socialism *(Sun–Thu 9am–3.45pm, Fri 9–1.30pm)*. All visits to Mount Zion are free of charge.

CHAGALL WINDOWS (0) (🗺 0)

Marc Chagall created 12 windows dedicated to the 12 tribes of Israel for the synagogue in the Hadassah Medical Center in the En Kerem district. The windows have become a major tourist attraction. *Sun–Thu 8am–1.15pm and 2pm–3.30pm | Hadassah Hospital, En Kerem, entrance: Kennedy Building | www.hadassah.org.il | entrance fee 10 NIS*

DAVID'S CITADEL (TOWER OF DAVID) (U C4) (🗺 c4)

In 1967, archaeologists discovered that the foundation walls of what had been previously known as 'Herod's Palace' came from a period long before the time of Christ. Sultan Suleiman had the fortress that Emperor Hadrian had destroyed reconstructed in the 15th century but the minaret was not completed until as late as 1665. The citadel *(Tower of David)* houses the *Museum of the History of Jerusalem* and 🔆 there is a wonderful view over the Old Town from the tower. *Sun–Thu 10am–5pm, Fri 10am–2pm | entrance fee 30 NIS, audio guide: 10 NIS, son et lumière: 55 NIS | tel. 02 6 26 53 33 | www.towerofdavid.org.il*

CHURCH OF THE REDEEMER 🔆 (U D4) (🗺 d4)

Emperor Wilhelm II made an endowment so that the *Church of the Redeemer* could be built near the Church of the Holy Sepulchre and assure a Protestant presence in the Holy City; today, it is the centre for Jerusalem's Lutherans. The unique view from the top of the 46m (150ft)-high tower makes up for all the effort necessary to climb it. *Mon–Thu, Sat 9am–1pm and 1.30–3pm | tower 4 NIS*

CHURCH OF THE HOLY SEPULCHRE ★ (U C–D4) (🗺 c–d4)

For 1700 years, Christians have come from all over the world to the place where, according to their belief, Jesus' destiny was fulfilled – his self-sacrifice on the Cross, his entombment and finally the Resurrection. To satisfy a wish made by his mother Helena, Emperor Constantine had a church built on Mount Golgotha in 326; it received its present form from the crusaders in the year 1149. Cramped in between the bazaar, monasteries and

In the struggle for the best places in the church, the Armenians, Catholics and Greek Orthodox were awarded the main nave, the Copts, Ethiopians and Syrian Jacobites the side aisles and galleries. Only the Holy Sepulchre in the centre of the church belongs to all six. In order to

Marc Chagall created the beautiful windows in the synagogue of the Hadassah Hospital

chapels, the Church of the Holy Sepulchre – with its beautiful stone carvings on the entrance façade – can only really be seen from the church forecourt. Several storeys high and often rather convoluted, its interior provides space for 30 chapels shared between six Christian confessions (Armenian, Ethiopian, Greek Orthodox, Roman Catholic, Coptic and Syrian Jacobite). Endless disputes between the confessions led to centuries of contesting over the true faith, conflicts between the confessions in the church and the veneration of a mass of various saints.

stop the strife, Sultan Suleiman gave the power of the keys to a Moslem family in Jerusalem in the 12th century. To the present day, their descendants have the responsibility of opening the portal of the church every morning and closing it in the evening. Several male members of each confession remain in the church overnight.

The Holy Sepulchre itself is at the centre of the church. A narrow passages leads from here to the tomb that is only illuminated by candles. There are usually long queues waiting to get in as only five people are allowed to be inside the chamber at any one time.

A tour of the Church of the Holy Sepulchre is like wandering through a labyrinth of overladen religiosity. If you don't want to cavations from the time of the Second Temple. *Visits only on guided tours | reservations only through Western Wall Heritage Foundation, tel. 02 6 27 13 33 | www.thekotel.org*

Church of the Holy Sepulchre: the Anointing Stone symbolises the 13th Station of the Cross

lose track of things, you should take part in a guided tour or not visit the church until late in the afternoon when there are only a few people praying there. The Catholic Franciscans celebrate mass every day at 4pm in the chapel and then make a solemn candle-lit procession through the church. *Daily Sept–May 5am–7pm, June–Aug 4am–8pm | free admission*

INSIDER TIP **HASMONEAN TUNNEL**
(U D3–4) (*ᗰ d3–4*)
Subterranean passages along the Temple Mount walls *(Western Wall Tunnel)* between the Western Wall and Via Dolorosa. Extremely interesting archaeological ex-

HERODIAN QUARTER – THE WOHL MUSEUM AND BURNT HOUSE
(U D4) (*ᗰ d4*)
Religious and household articles from the time of the Second Temple, in the Old City house of a rich Jerusalem family destroyed by the Romans in 70AD and excavated and reconstructed in 1970. Audiovisual presentations. *Sun–Thu 9am–5pm, Fri 9am–1pm | Hakaraim Street | Jewish Quarter | www.rova-yehudi.org.il | entrance fee 15 NIS*

ISRAEL MUSEUM ● (0) (*ᗰ 0*)
The Israel Museum is the largest and most important in the country and consists of

several departments including the Bezalel Art Museum, the Bronfman Archaeology and Bible Museum and the Billy Rose Art Garden with modern sculptures. The famous *Shrine of the Book* is especially impressive. This is where the scrolls with the oldest Bible texts from the Book of Isaiah discovered in Qumran in 1947 are displayed. This is complemented by unique exhibits from the time of Jesus and early Christianity, as well as an open-air model of Jerusalem (on a scale of 1:50) in the Roman period that makes the dominant position of the Temple Mount and the Second Temple immediately apparent. Temporary special exhibitions and activities for children. *Mon, Wed, Thu, Sat, Sun 10am–5pm, Tue 4–9pm, Fri 10am–2pm | Ruppin St. | Givat Ram, opposite the Knesset | www.imj.org.il | entrance fee 36 NIS*

JEWISH QUARTER ⭐
(U D4) *(ⵍ d4)*

This quarter was painstakingly reconstructed to old plans after East Jerusalem had been captured in the Six Day War. Today, around 700 Jewish families and Yeshiva students live here – most of them in their own expensive flats. Foreigners and non-Jewish Israelis are not allowed to move into the Jewish Quarter as the purchaser must have a family, live permanently in the flat and be liable to perform Israeli military service. In spite of the strict Sabbath rules, the Quarter is quite different from Mea Shearim. Here, visitors find pleasant teahouses and cafés, shops and interesting architecture on every corner. In addition, no other district of the Old City has as many museums as the Jewish Quarter. The excavated and ideally restored *Cardo*, the main north-south road with the underground sewers of Roman Jerusalem, cuts through the Quarter. There is a model of the Quarter in Roman times on display in the *Cardo Information Centre* which is open to all. The new *Hurva Synagogue*, which was reconstructed in 2008 with a massive supporting arch from the old building that was destroyed in 1948, is well worth visiting. A visit to the *Herodian Quarter Museum* with the so-called 'Burnt House' is another must.

WESTERN WALL ⭐ ●
(U D4) *(ⵍ d4)*

Since the destruction of Jerusalem by the Romans under Emperor Titus in 70AD and their following expulsion, the Western Wall *(Wailing Wall)*, the most sacred place for Jews, has symbolised their longing to return to Jerusalem and ultimately for a state of their own. On the Sabbath, particularly religious believers gather here in front of the gigantic limestone blocks. The Wailing Wall was once the outer western wall of the temple district, not the Temple itself. It has borne its name since the destruction of the Second Temple.

It is necessary to keep your head covered when you visit the Wall because the forecourt is considered a synagogue. Since 1970, the High Rabbinate has succeeded in having men and women separated when they pray at the Wall. Western Wall etiquette: visitors are permitted to come close to the wall although people are praying there, but they should not smoke, should turn off their mobile phones, not talk to each other, not light any candles and not take photographs on the Sabbath. People praying at the wall take on different postures: Christians usually pray standing still or kneeling; Moslems alone or in groups moving according to a prescribed ritual, while pious Jews get into the appropriate mood for praying through intense movements. These are in keeping with the verse from the Psalms: 'All my bones shall say, LORD who is like unto thee!' (Psalm 35).

Everyday life in the quarter of the 'Hundred Doors' reminds one of how things were in a schtetl in East Europe in the 18th and 19th centuries. The people living here are particularly pious Jews who follow the law *(Haredim)*; most of them live from religious teaching and donations (e.g.

Thursday. Visitors are free to move around in the quarter. However, signs let them know that decent clothing is desired and that the Sabbath laws must be respected.

MENACHIM BEGIN MUSEUM
(U C5) (🗺 c5)

This museum is devoted to the life of the sixth Israeli Prime Minister and documents

Western Wall: this is where the faithful converse with God

social security benefits). Life follows the established paths of the true faith in this quarter established between Haneriim, Mea Shearim and Shmuel Salant Streets outside the Old City in 1874. Many of the inhabitants of Mea Shearim consider the State of Israel blasphemous as, in their opinion, only the Messiah has the right to create a Jewish state. The Sabbath is observed very strictly and therefore there is great activity while preparations are being made until late in the night on

his career starting with his underground activities. Many old photographs as well as a reconstruction of his humble house in Tel Aviv. *Sun–Thu 9am–4.30pm, Fri 9am–12.30pm | Nachon Street 6, opposite the Cinemateque | www.begincenter.org.il | entrance fee 15 NIS*

MUSEUM OF ISLAMIC ART
(0) (🗺 0)

This museum displays beautiful objects from the world of Islam; mainly arts and crafts with especially noteworthy jewellery and carpet departments. *Sun, Mon, Wed 10am–3pm, Tue and Thu 10am–6pm, Fri/Sat 10am–2pm | Hapalmach Street 2 | www.islamicart.co.il | entrance fee 20 NIS*

MOUNT OF OLIVES ★
(U F3–4) (🗺 f3–4)

On the eastern side, opposite the Old City but separated from it by the Kidron Valley, lies a hill where the gnarled olive trees that gave it its name still grow in the ● *Garden of Gethsemane*. The garden is a place of tranquillity. Narrow gravel paths have been laid out between the impressive olive trees; the size of their trunks gives an idea of how old they really are. Low lattice fences remind visitors not to go off the paths and guards also makes sure that only a limited number of visitors are in the garden at any one time so that peace and quiet can be maintained. On the INSIDER TIP ▶ path from St Stephan's Gate to the Mount of Olives, visitors pass several churches named after biblical happenings: the *Church of All Nations* (also known as the *Church of the Agony*), the *Monastery Church Dominus Flevit* (where Jesus lamented the fate of Jerusalem), the Russian Orthodox *Maria Magdalene Church* with its golden onion towers, the

Chapel of the Ascension (built by Wilhelm II in 1910; re-consecrated after renovation in 1990) and the *Paternoster Church* (it is said that this is where Jesus taught the apostles the Lord's Prayer). The 🔆 *Hotel Seven Arches* on the top of the Mount of Olives has seen better days but it still provides its guests with the most beautiful view of the Old City. Especially in the morning, the sun lights up the golden cupola of the Dome of the Rock to create the perfect picture postcard photo.

Many pious Jews have their graves on the western slope of the Mount of Olives because they believe that when the Messiah arrives he will enter the walled city with all of the resurrected and hold the Last Judgement. Burials have taken place in the oldest cemetery in Jerusalem since the days of King David. The limestone makes it easy to dig graves and a stony sea of tombs stretches up the Kidron Valley as far as the Hotel Seven arches: some high sarcophaguses, some simple flat slabs. People looking for a specific grave have to know their way around; there are no paths, the inscriptions have often faded and many grave slabs are broken. Mere mortals have absolutely no chance of being buried here. Only personalities like Israel's Prime Minister Menachem Begin can find their final resting place in this cemetery al-

GOD'S LETTERBOX

If you get close enough to the Western Wall, you will see that there are small slips of paper *(kvittelchen)* stuck between the mighty blocks of stone. They contain appeals and wishes to the Lord. Those who are not able to put a letter into God's 'letterbox' – because they live abroad, for example – can send a letter, fax or email to the Jerusalem rabbinate – a rabbi then acts as the courier. Of course, God's letterbox has to be cleared from time to time and the rabbinate has the *kvittelchen* taken out of the slits at night every two weeks or so and 'buries' them anonymously on the Mount of Olives.

though, in recent years, victims of terrorist attacks were also laid to rest in it.

The Golden Gate, through which the Messiah will enter the city with the resurrected, is opposite the Mount of Olives. To prevent this happening, the Moslems bricked up the gate and established a Moslem cemetery in front of it in the 7th century *(the Jewish cemetery is open from sunrise to sunset)*.

ROCKEFELLER MUSEUM
(U E2) *(⌕ e2)*

The museum is funded by the Rockefeller Foundation and shows important archaeological finds from local excavations. *Sun–Thu 10am–3pm, Sat 10am–2pm | Suleiman St. 27, corner of Jericho Rd. | free admission*

THE SECURITY WALL IN EAST
JERUSALEM ● (0) *(⌕ 0)*

East Jerusalem, which was occupied in 1967 and annexed in breach of international law in 1980, has now expanded far beyond the city limits and 'grown' into West Jordan. In order to protect it from Islamic suicide attacks and Arab terrorists, Israel has now massively extended its 'Anti-terror Security Wall' in East Jerusalem. In the village of El Tur to the east of the Mount of Olives, it is possible to walk or drive to the 7.5m (25ft)-high concrete wall with barbed wire and watchtowers that stretches for miles through the landscape. The graffiti on the wall gives visitors an idea of what the Palestinian families who are forced to live separated from their relatives on the other side of the wall think of this gigantic, impenetrable concrete cordon. In the meantime, 'The Wall' has become an 'attraction' in Jerusalem – just as it used to be in Berlin. *Starting from the Mount of Olives, past the Carmelite Convent and down the village street to the turning space in front of the wall*

VIA DOLOROSA
(U C–D 3–4) *(⌕ c–d 3–4)*

Once a year, at Easter, the series of narrow streets in Jerusalem's Old City that are known as the 'Via Dolorosa' are the scene of an impressive display of devout religiosity. Thousands of believers follow the Way of the Cross past the 14 stations from the court (at St Stephen's Gate) to the place of crucifixion at Golgotha (Church of the Holy Sepulchre). The strongest male pilgrims carry a wooden cross. The Arab and Christian sections of the Old City reverberate with song, laments and prayers.

This is especially impressive on Good Friday but visitors can experience a smaller version in the procession of the Franciscans every Friday. Those who want to bear a cross can hire one at the entrance to the Church of the Holy Sepulchre; Palestinian lads carry it to the first station the 'Place of Condemnation' in what is today the El Omariya School. *Procession Fri 3pm (in summer 4pm)*

You will also encounter individual groups of pilgrims with heavy wooden crosses who stop and sing and pray at all of the stations during the week. Each station is named after a specific event in the Passion of Christ.

For Christians, the Via Dolorosa is the holiest road on earth. However, there is no historical or archaeological assurance that this is actually the Way of the Cross. It was not until the 13th century, and after long-drawn-out negotiations, that the Christian confessions agreed on establishing the present route with the 14 stations as the authentic one, although only eight are actually mentioned in the Bible. Since the 14th century, the *Custodia Terrae Sanctae* (Custody of the Holy Land) has been firmly in the hands of Catholic Franciscans and the monks in their brown habits are therefore responsible for the processions on the Via Dolorosa. The faithful stand in front of the stations marked with Roman numerals, the accompanying priest reads the appropriate section from the Gospel – often with the help of a megaphone – and the group then launches into a hymn.

INSIDER TIP ▶ ABU SHUKRI
(U D3) (*ф d3*)

The best Arab restaurant in the Old City, excellent cooking (the best humus in town), friendly, speedy service. *Daily 8am–*

The Hall of Remembrance is the centre of the Yad Vashem memorial

YAD VASHEM ★
(0) (*ф 0*)

National Israeli memorial site in memory of the 6 million European Jews murdered by the National Socialists during World War II. A museum documents the persecution of the Jews in Europe – from being deprived of their rights, their ghettoising, to their industrially organised murder. *Sun–Wed 9am–5pm, Thu 9am–8pm, Fri 9am–2pm, closed Sat and Jewish holidays | Hazikkarm Street Mount Herzl | www.yad vashem.org | free admission*

5.30pm | Al Wad St. 63, opposite the 5th station on the Via Dolorosa | tel. 02 6 27 15 38 | Moderate

ARABESQUE
(U D1) (*ф d1*)

Guests can choose between the garden restaurant under the trees in the inner courtyard and the elegant restaurant on the ground floor – both serve the same excellent Swiss cuisine with traces of the Orient. In winter, you should have one for the road in the cellar bar (a former prison);

in summer, the garden lounge is the right choice. Extremely exclusive atmosphere; reservations essential. *Daily | America Colony Hotel | Nablus Road | tel. 02 6 27 97 77 | Expensive*

EL DORADO CAFÉ (U D2) (*ₘ d2*)
Superior Palestinian café, excellent coffee from espresso to latte macchiato as well as light dishes, cakes and ice cream. It is also possibly to take away freshly roasted coffee. *Daily 7am–10pm | Salah Eddin Street 19 | tel. 02 6 26 09 93 | www.izhiman.com | Budget*

INSIDER TIP ▸ KING'S GARDEN ☼ (U B4) (*ₘ b4*)
Exquisite restaurant in the King David Hotel with a wonderful view of the Old City. Light, tasty meals from the cuisines of all of the peoples living in Israel. *Daily 10am–11.30pm | King David St. 23 | tel. 02 6 20 88 88 | Expensive*

ROOF TOP ☼ ● (U C3) (*ₘ c3*)
Wine and cheese, as well as snacks, but mainly a magnificent view over the Old City. Communicative guests, roof terrace of the Notre Dame of Jerusalem Center. *Daily 6pm–midnight | Hatzanhanim St. | Moderate*

INSIDER TIP ▸ THREE ARCHES ☼ (U B4) (*ₘ b4*)
Terrace restaurant in the hotel of the same name, international cuisine, excellent teas, cheerful atmosphere, even more cheerful service. *Daily 7am–11pm | King David Street 26 | tel. 02 5 69 26 92 | Moderate*

INSIDER TIP ▸ TICHO HOUSE (U B3) (*ₘ b3*)
The former home of the painter Anna Ticho was one of the first houses outside the walled Old City and is now a wonderful garden restaurant and museum café.

Small meat dishes, excellent fish and many vegetarian specialities. Various exhibitions also held. *Sun–Thu 10am–midnight, Fri 9am–3pm, Sat 7pm–midnight | Harav Kook St. 9 | tel. 02 6 24 41 86 | www.go-out.com/ticho | Moderate*

SHOPPING

AHAVA ⊙ (U B–C4) (*ₘ b–c4*)
Spacious shop in the new Mamilla Passage with exclusive cosmetic products made with natural minerals from the Dead Sea. *Alrov Mamilla Ave. | Sun–Thu 10am–6pm, Fri 10am–4pm*

BAZAAR (U C–D4) (*ₘ c–d4*)
The most traditional souk in the Middle East stretches between Damascus Gate and Jaffa Gate in the Christian and Moslem quarters of the Old City. With its great variety of souvenirs, Roman amphorae, oil lamps and mementos of the Holy City, along with T-shirts and the like, it has regained its old atmosphere although it is not visited by as many foreign tourists as it was before the Second Intifada. *Daily 10am–sunset, some shops stay open longer, others are closed Fri*

HUTZOT HAYOTZER (U C4) (*ₘ c4*)
Large artists' centre with many small shops, studios and galleries selling modern Israeli arts and crafts. *Below Jaffa Gate | Sun–Thu 10am–5pm, Fri 10am–2pm*

JERUSALEM MALL ● (0) (*ₘ 0*)
There are now even gigantic American-style shopping arcades in Jerusalem and this one is the largest and most interesting of all. The Israelis call it the Kanyon Yerushalayim or Malcha. The multi-storey gallery is flooded with light and has around 300 shops and more than 30 cafés and restaurants including some fast-food chains. A wide range of elegant clothing,

jewellery and electronic goods (with a 16% VAT refund). *Next to Teddy Kollek Stadium | Sun–Thu 9.30am–10pm, Fri 9.30am–3pm*

MAMILLA (U B–C4) (*⌂ b–c4*)

The shopping street *Alrov Mamilla Avenue* with its many cafés has been established as a pedestrian precinct in the restored historical Mamilla Quarter below the French St Vincent de Paul Convent.

magazine 'Time-out Israel', provide information on lectures, films, cabaret theatres and *concerts of religious music in the Church of the Redeemer. Ben Yehuda Street* is especially lively in the evening.

INSIDER TIP **CELLAR BAR** (U C1) (*⌂ c1*)

The bar in the American Colony Hotel is in a 130-year-old cellar. The bartender is the best-informed person in Jerusalem as

Damascus Gate: business is flourishing here near the main entrance to the Old City

ENTERTAINMENT

There is not much room for worldly entertainment in the Holy City and the possibilities for enjoying yourself in the evening are completely different in Israeli West Jerusalem and the Palestinian districts in the east of the city. The weekend editions of the English 'Jerusalem Post' and 'Ha'aretz' newspapers that are published on Friday, as well as the monthly event

the hotel is where UN diplomats stay. *Daily 8pm–3am | tel. 02 6 27 97 77*

INSIDER TIP **KHAN ZAMAN**
(U D1) (*⌂ d1*)

Even if you're in West Jerusalem, you should make a visit to the popular NGO rendezvous in the Jerusalem Hotel. *Daily 6pm–midnight | Nablus Road, behind Damascus Gate | beer 10 NIS, coffee 6 NIS, hookah 20 NIS*

THREE ARCHES (U B4) (*🗺 b4*)

Those interested in excellent folkloric dancing and singing, concerts, guest theatre performance and readings (in English) should take a look at the regular events in the historical *YMCA building. Programme and dates www.jerusalemymca.org or in the daily newspapers | King David St. 26 | usually free admission*

coloured Bisazza mosaic tiling, modern fitness centre, spa complex with many facilities to make you feel good. A 'Leading Hotel of the World' under Swiss management, international guests, very popular with western journalists. *98 rooms | Louis Vincent Street 1 | tel. 02 6 27 97 77 | www.americancolony.com | Expensive*

American Colony: live like a pasha

WHERE TO STAY

The Jerusalem Hotel association *(www. jerusalem-hotels.org.il)* provides an overview of hotels in the city.

AMERICAN COLONY ★ ●
(U C1) (*🗺 c1*)

The most beautiful hotel in Israel is located the former city palais of a pasha and has an attractive inner courtyard, lovely garden, spacious rooms and perfect service. Oriental luxury combined with the greatest efficiency in a relaxed atmosphere. New pool with turquoise-

BEIT SHMUEL (U B4) (*🗺 b4*)

Hotel and youth hostel rolled into one with a great deal of comfort near the Old City; high standards, operated by 'Mercaz Shimshon' (Reform Judaism). *250 beds in 40 rooms (including 12 elegant double rooms) | Eliahu Shamau St. 6, corner of King David St. 13 | tel. 02 6 20 34 55 | www. bshmuel-hotel.com | Moderate*

YITZHAK RABIN YOUTH HOSTEL
(O) (*🗺 o*)

New, comfortable youth hostel. 77 rooms with bath and WC, air-conditioning, some with television. Check in from 3pm.

Nachman Avigad 1, corner of Yehuda Burla | tel. 02 6 78 01 01 | rabin@iyha.org.il | Budget

KING DAVID HOTEL (U B4) (*b4*)

The city's most traditional hotel that has hosted almost all of the world's important statesmen. Here, all of the guests' wishes are met. In 1946, the west wing was blown up by the Jewish terror group Irgun because it housed the British headquarters. The King David is the most renowned of the 'Leading Hotels of the World' in Israel. *257 rooms | King David Street 23 | tel. 02 6 20 88 88 | www.danhotels.com | Expensive*

LUTHERAN GUESTHOUSE (U C4) (*c4*)

The guesthouse and youth hostel run by the Evangelical Church in the heart of the Old City can only be reached on foot. German management, beautiful inner courtyard, charming garden, open-minded guests. *23 rooms | Jaffa Gate | St Mark's Rd. | tel. 02 6 26 68 88 | www.luth-guesthouse-jerusalem.com | Moderate*

INSIDER TIP NOTRE DAME OF JERUSALEM CENTER (U C3) (*c3*)

Impressive palatial building from the 19th century on the edge of the Old City opposite the New Gate, owned by the Vatican. This was once a hostel for pilgrims but today its doors are also open to other guests. All the rooms are functionally furnished, painstakingly renovated in 2011. *140 rooms | Hatzanhanim St. | tel. 02 6 27 91 11 | www.notredamecenter.org | Moderate*

INSIDER TIP AUSTRIAN HOSPICE (U D3) (*d3*)

You can be the Archbishop of Vienna's guest in the middle of the Old City of Jerusalem. Very pleasant building, newly furnished rooms, beautiful garden. *18 rooms and several dormitories | Via Dolorosa 37, opposite Station 3 | tel. 02 6 26 58 00 | www.austrianhospice.com | Moderate*

YMCA – THREE ARCHES (U B4) (*b4*)

Today, this Christian-operated social centre with a swimming pool, library and lecture halls also has a restaurant and hotel with many amenities. The building has an interesting history: General Allenby lived here in 1933. The ✺ *YMCA Tower*, from where visitors have a spectacular view over Jerusalem is part of the complex. *(Visit to the tower by lift also for non-residents, daily 8am–8pm | 5 NIS). 66 rooms | King David St. 26 | tel. 02 5 69 26 92 | www.ymca3arch.co.il | Moderate*

LOW BUDGET

▶ The volunteers from *Sandeman's New Europe Tours* organise free tours through the Old Town of Jerusalem – with a pro-Israeli slant. None of the important sights are omitted on the 4-hour tour. *Meeting point: daily 11am | Jaffa Gate | tips accepted | www.neweuropetours.eu*

▶ The Israeli parliament, the ● *Knesset*, is the scene of heated debates about the future of the country. The large, flat functional building in the western section of the city was planned by Josef Klarwein and built between 1960 and 1966; the Rothschild family footed the bill. A visit including a tour in English is free of charge. You have to show your passport. *Sun, Thu 8.30am–2.30pm | www.knesset.gov.il*

INFORMATION

CHRISTIAN INFORMATION CENTRE
(U C4) (🗺 c4)

Information on all Christian institutions, places of pilgrimage and Christian guesthouses. *Jaffa Gate | tel. 02 6 27 26 92 | Mon–Fri 8.30am–5.30pm, Sat 8.30m–12.30pm | www.cicts.org*

TOURIST INFORMATION CENTER
(U C4) (🗺 c4)

Jaffa Gate | tel. 02 6 28 03 82 | Sun–Thu 8.30am–12.45pm | www.jerusalem.muni. il. Informative material and maps of the city.

INSIDER TIP ▶ UNITED NATIONS
(U C1) (🗺 c1)

The 'Office for the Coordination of Humanitarian Affairs – occupied Palestinian territory (OCHA-oPt) provides up-to-date UN material as well as maps of the occupied Palestinian territories with the course of the wall and its checkpoints. *St George 7 | tel. 02 5 82 99 62 | www.ochaopt.org*

WHERE TO GO

The following destinations are all on the so-called West Bank, the area to the west of the River Jordan that was Jordanian territory in the period between the end of the British mandate and the Six Day War in 1967, which the Arab League then handed over to the Palestinians at the Rabat Conference in 1974 to make it possible for them to establish an independent state. It is almost completely identical with the area that the 1947 UN separation plan foresaw for the Arab population of the British mandate territory. Since 1967, Israel abolished all of the borders to the West Bank and moved the frontier with Jordan to the east of the Jordan River. This makes it possible for tourists to visit all of the important sites on this side of the

THROUGH JERUSALEM BY TRAM

Jerusalem has had a user and environmentally-friendly public transport system since 2010 – the Jerusalem Light Rail. Construction of this streamlined, modern tram took more than 10 years. The line crosses the spectacular new Chords Bridge that the Spanish specialist in the field, Santiago Calatrava, designed especially for the Light Rail and takes 45 mins. for the 14km (9mi) through Jerusalem from Mount Herzl in the west, along Jaffa Street, past the Old City in annexed East Jerusalem, to the Jewish settlement Pisgat Zeev far in the north. This settlement is in the Jerusalem section of occupied West Jordan and has led to problems for some time; the Arab league accuses Israel of using the tramline to stress its claim to all of Jerusalem. For this reason, on the day the Jerusalem tram started operating, Saudi Arabia cancelled its contract with the French tramline company for the billion-dollar project to build a line between Mecca and Medina. It is still peaceful but the Jerusalem city council is taking precautions: to make sure that there is no hostility between Orthodox Jewish and Arab passengers there are always security personnel on the trams *(Sun–Thu 5.30am–11.30pm, every 10 mins. | www.citypass.co.il | fare: 4 NIS).*

river from Jerusalem. Israel's border, which has been recognised by international law since 1949, is now known as the 'green border'. For some time now, Israel has been erecting a concrete wall with watchtowers that is, in places, 7.5m (25-foot)-high, along this boundary and far into the Palestinian West Bank that can only be passed at a few checkpoints after time-consuming controls (see p. 76).

The West Bank is the Palestinians' core country. In official communiqués and on maps, Israel consciously uses the old biblical names for these Palestinian territories: *Samara* for the areas north of Jerusalem and *Judea* for those in the south. There are so-called 'A Zones' within the West Bank. These are 'islands' that the Palestinians administer themselves although access is completely controlled by Israel. The following towns of Bethlehem, Hebron, Jericho and Ramallah belong to these A Zones. On principle, Israeli taxis do not travel into the A Zones; that means not even to Bethlehem. It is therefore advisable to make the trip with a taxi from East Jerusalem or with a tour operator.

BETHLEHEM
(125 D2) (*ØJ E7*)

Bethlehem (Bayt Lahm) lies in a picturesque hilly landscape only 11km (7mi) south of Jerusalem. Most of the people living in the town where King David and Jesus were born are Palestinian Christians and it is also under Palestinian administration.

The tourist centre of Bethlehem is the *Church of the Nativity*, built by Emperor Constantine, on Manger Square. *Rachel's Tomb* – she was Jacob's wife – is on the road into the town. Christians who believe in miracles like to visit the *Lactation Grotto Church*. It was built where it is said that the Virgin Mary lost a drop of milk while she was nursing Jesus and that

Everyday life in the Old Town of Bethlehem

the rocks then changed their colour to dazzling white. The annual highlight in Bethlehem comes with the procession followed by midnight mass held in the Nativity Church to celebrate Christmas.

HEBRON
(125 D3) (*Ø D7*)

Hebron (Al Halil) is one of the oldest, continuously inhabited, cities in the world; it is 35km (22mi) south of Jerusalem. 150,000 Arabs live here in the centre of the mountains of Judea, which are controlled by the Israelis, surrounded by beautiful old vineyards. *Abraham's Tomb* lies in the *Cave of Machpela* in the very heart of Hebron. Both Jews and Moslems revere this site. Jewish settlers, led by Moshe Levinger from the USA, moved into three houses nearby in 1979; until today, they live behind a high fence protected by Israeli soldiers. This section of the town is not administered by the Palestinians. Hebron is one of the places where visitors are confronted first-hand with the frontlines of the Jewish-Palestinian conflict.

In 1970, the Jewish village of *Kiryat Arba* was established above Hebron; today 1000 religiously fanatical families live here. In 1994, Baruch Goldstein from Kiryat Arba shot 35 Palestinians praying in the Machpela Mosque.

JERICHO ★
(125 E2) (*Ø E6*)

Everyone knows the story of the biblical trumpets whose overpowering sound brought the walls of Jericho tumbling down in 1300BC. Jericho (Yeriho; pop. 20,000) was the capital city of the nascent Palestinian state from 1994 to 1999.

The many freshwater springs assure exceptionally productive cultivation in the banana, date and orange plantations surrounding the city. Shady streets and Arab cafés invite visitors to take a break. The ruins of *Hisham Palace* and biblical Jericho *(Tell es Sultan)* are located 3km (under 2mi) to the north of the city *(daily 8am–5pm | entrance fee 10 NIS)*. Excavations show that Jericho was destroyed – and rebuilt – 20 times in the 10,000 years of its history. A INSIDER TIP cablecar *(telle-pherique)* at Tell es Sultan takes visitors up to the *Mount of Temptation* with its caves where Jesus fasted and prayed for 40 days and nights *(runs daily, 9am–4pm | 40 NIS)*. The monastery commemorating this hangs like a swallow's nest on the slopes of the mountain that plummet perpendicularly into the valley below. There is a restaurant on the terrace at the top station that opens up wonderful views over Jericho.

INSIDER TIP ▶ RAMALLAH
(125 D1) (*Ø E6*)

The climatic health resort Ramallah (Ram Allah; pop. 60,000) is only a stone's throw from Jerusalem at an altitude of 870m (2850ft) above sea level. The town ('God's Hill') used to be a popular holiday destination for wealthy Jordanians. It was placed under Palestinian autonomy in 1995 and has been the administrative capital of the future Palestinian state since 1999. This is also where the offices of the Palestinian president, the so-called *Muccada,* can be found. Yassir Arafat was buried on the grounds in November 2004. Tourists arriving from Jerusalem have to undergo rigorous security checks at the Qalandia Checkpoint in the south of Ramallah. Especially 'when leaving the country', there are long queues of cars waiting here because a time-consuming check is made of every single one of them. Bus passengers have to cross the border on foot. Ramallah is booming. There are many new buildings and houses, cultural activities, cafés, hotels and possibilities to go out and have fun; the town's streets are full of life. The economic upswing is mainly as result of the generosity of international donor countries. This has made Ramallah the most attractive place for Palestinians on the West Bank. But, when one is in Ramallah, one hears that it is actually a 'five-star prison' where all forms of access, all flows of money and goods, water, electricity and all transport are subjected to Israel and its restrictions. Many European NGOs have their diplomatic representation in the Palestinian autonomous territory.

After around three hours, hikers arrive at **INSIDER TIP** *St George's Monastery* that was founded in the 5th century and is now in the care of Greek Orthodox monks. It is built like a cluster of swallows' nests on the precipitous rockface – a really impressive

The water for St George's Monastery comes from Wadi Qelt

WADI QELT AND ST GEORGE'S MONASTERY (125 D2) (*𝄞 E6*)

Half way along the main road from Jerusalem to Jericho, you can have yourself dropped off at the carpark (signposted) at the entrance to Wadi Qelt and hike along well-marked paths through the wild, rugged rocky canyon. At some places, you will also see the impressive remains of the Herodian aqueduct.

image of monastic seclusion. The monastery was destroyed by Persian troops in 614 and reconstructed in its present form in the 19th century. The skulls of the monk murdered by the Persians are laid out in a glass sarcophagus in the chapel. There is a path from the monastery to Jericho. *Sun–Fri 6am–5pm (winter 8am–3pm), Sat 6am–noon, Thu morning service at 5am*

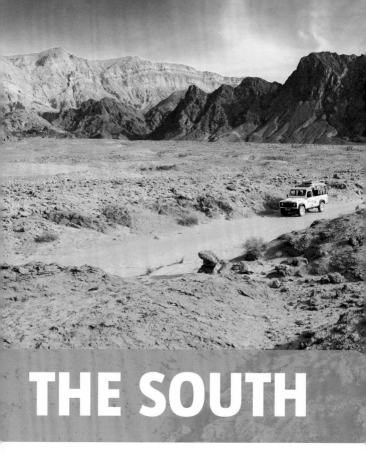

THE SOUTH

The south of Israel: that is the Negev Desert with fantastic stone formations, bizarre canyons, enormous sand dunes – a landscape of unspoilt nature. The best way to experience the region is by bus or car; there are only a few roads, but they are in excellent condition.

The wild, deserted Negev is the perfect place for jeep tours. The lowest point on the face of the earth, the Dead Sea, is at the northeastern edge of the desert region. It is only a 2½-hour drive from here to the southernmost point in Israel on the Red Sea. This is the site of Eilat, a stronghold for seaside holidays, windsurfers and divers. Eilat is not only the most popular

seaside resort in Israel with its own airport and dozens of big hotels, it is also the starting point for day-trips to Jordan (to Petra and Wadi Rum, for example) and to the Egyptian Sinai Peninsula.

BEERSHEBA

(124 B–C4) (*ɖ C–D8*) **The industrial and university town and 'capital' of the Negev is one of the Israeli cities with the highest increase in population.**

1948: 2000 inhabitants, in 2010 more than 200,000 – mainly Russian immigrants. Once upon a time, Abraham en-

Photo: Desert landscape near Eilat

Between the Dead and the Red Seas –
the Negev Desert in the south covers almost
half the territory of the State of Israel

countered Abimelech in Beersheba (Be'er
Sheva) (Genesis: 21, 22) and that led to
the name of the city: 'Well of the Oath'.

SIGHTSEEING

ABRAHAM'S WELL

This well was the reason the patriarch
settled here 3700 years ago – its present
form comes from the Turkish period. *Sun–*
Thu 9am–4pm, Fri 8am–noon | Hebron
Rd. 1 | entrance fee 10 NIS

BEDOUIN MARKET

Thursday is market day and the market is
the city's main attraction. Starting at 6am,
Bedouins and merchants offer everything
imaginable on a large open square in the
south of the city: clothes and shoes, fruit
and groceries, antiques and new goods;

Canyons like this one, craters and wadis are characteristic of the Negev

the bargaining languages are Ivrit, Arabic and Russian!

BEN GURION UNIVERSITY
The university is the cultural centre of the city with music and theatre performances. Tours of the campus possible. *Ben Gurion St. | tel. 07 6 46 11 11 | www.bgu.ac.il*

MUSEUM OF BEDOUIN CULTURE – JOE ALON CENTER
Israel's most impressive museum of the Bedouin way of life; 17km (11mi) to the northeast in *Lahav Kibbutz. Sun–Thu 9am–5pm, Fri 9am–2pm | entrance fee 20 NIS*

TEL BEERSHEBA
The ruins of biblical Sheva lie 9km (6mi) to the east of Beersheba in a national park. It is said that Abraham lived here in this excavated city. There is an excellent view of the painstakingly restored walls of the fortifications, the storage and domestic houses, as well as the ancient roads, from the new observation tower. Tel Beersheba (together with other biblical Tels) has been a Unesco World Heritage Site since 2005. *Daily 8am–5pm (Oct–March 8am–4pm) | www.parks.org.il | entrance fee 14 NIS*

FOOD & DRINK

ACHUZAT SMILANSKI
Excellent food in an old renovated townhouse in the centre of the Old City. *Daily | Smilanski St. 23 | tel. 08 6 65 48 54 | www.rol.co.il | Moderate*

WHERE TO STAY

BET YAZIV
Long-standing youth hostel and educational centre in the heart of Beersheba. *80 beds in dormitories, 85 double rooms | Haatzmaut St. 79 | tel. 08 6 27 74 44 | Budget*

LEONARDO HOTEL NEGEV

Large, centrally located city hotel with swimming pool and considerable comfort – opened in 1996 as a Gold Tulip establishment and renovated in 2006. *256 rooms | Henrietta Sold St. 4 | tel. 08 6 40 54 44 | www.leonardo-hotels.com/israel-hotels/beer-sheva-hotels/leonardo-hotel-negev | Moderate*

TOURIST INFORMATION

Hebron Rd. 1, entrance to Abraham's Well | Tel. 08 6 23 46 13 | www.beer-sheva.muni.il

INSIDER TIP AVDAT (124 B6) *(𝄞 C–D10)*

The Nabataeans, whose most famous settlement was Petra in what is now Jordan, established the city of Avdat in the middle of the Negev in the 2nd century BC to protect their caravans on their way to the south. It was named after its builder King Obadas (Abdat) II. Avdat was destroyed in 106 but once again increased in significance under Byzantine rule around 400AD. Today, Avdat (En'Avedat) is a historical site with fascinating ruins. *(Daily 8am–5pm, Oct–March 4pm | tel. 08 6 55 15 11 | entrance fee 23 NIS)*. 50km (31mi) south of Beersheba on the road to Eilat.

MAMSHIT (124 C5) *(𝄞 D9)*

The second ruins of a Nabataean city named Mamshit lie in the eastern section of the Negev 40km (25mi) southeast of Beersheba near Dimona. It is the smallest Nabataean city in the Negev. Mainly ruins of domestic buildings and the streets between the different quarters have been excavated and restored in this 2000-year-old town. The floors of the churches erected around 500AD are decorated with coloured mosaics and Greek inscriptions.

The city of ruins lies in the *Mamshit National Park (daily 8am–5pm, Oct–March until 4pm | 08 6 55 64 78 | entrance fee 21 NIS | www.parks.org.il)*. The *Mamshit Camel Ranch* makes it possible to stay overnight in Bedouin tents and undertake excursions through the Negev on camels or in 4 × 4s *(30 rooms | tel. 08 9 43 68 82 | www.mamshit.co.il | Moderate)*.

NEGEV ★ (124–125 B–D 4–6, 126–127 B–D 1–6) *(𝄞 C–D 8–14)*

The Negev (Hebrew: 'south'): a desert of sand and stone (Arabic: An Naqb) with mountains, canyons and wadis covers almost half the surface area of Israel. People settled in this desert more than 3000 years ago as excavations, including those made in the Nabataean town of *Avdat*, show. The Negev was the place where nomadic Bedouins lived until modern times. Today, there are more 50 permanently lived-in towns and villages in the Negev; the most important are Arad and Beersheba but the most impressive is *Mispe Ramon* on the rim of the Ramon Crater *(Makhtesh)*.

★ Negev
Through the desert by jeep or on a camel → p. 89

★ Underwater Observatory Marine Park
Submarine encounters → p. 91

★ Masada
The battle for the fortress near the Dead Sea became a legend → p. 93

★ Dead Sea
Effortless swimming → p. 95

In Eilat, people get together in the evening for a game of backgammon near the sea

A jeep tour through the Negev followed by dinner around a campfire before spending the night under the stars is an unforgettable experience. Information from *Desert Adventures Israel | www.gonegev.co.il*

EILAT

(126 C6) *(ꭥ D14)* **The main reason for most people travelling to the south to Eilat (pop. 50,000) is to go swimming. The more than 50 hotels in all price categories, half of them on the beach and most with all-inclusive facilities, have made Eilat Israel's number-one seaside holiday resort. But, Eilat also has a history.** This is where King Solomon met the Queen of Sheba, it was a Roman stronghold, the Crusaders – and later, the Turks – fought battles here. Eilat has belonged to Israel since 1949. The old airport is in the centre of town; most of the expensive hotels are on the North Beach. The border crossing

to Egypt is 9km (6mi) to the south in *Taba (tel. 08 6 37 01 92)* and tourists can enter Jordanian *Aqaba (tel. 08 6 30 05 55)* at Checkpoint Arava a few miles north.

SIGHTSEEING

DOLPHIN REEF

Dolphins and sea lions live in their natural environment in this complex on the shore of the Red Sea. A special attraction: you can get close to the dolphins in the pools. Experienced attendants help the guests do this. *Daily 9am–5pm | Southern Beach (bus line 15) | tel. 07 6 37 59 35 | www. dolphinreef.co.il | entrance fee 64 NIS*

KING'S CITY

Amusement park in an exotic palace complex with waterfalls, caves and biblical adventures at the end of the promenade to the west of the Eastern Lagoon. *Daily 10am–8pm | tel. 08 6 30 44 44 | www. kingscity.co.il | 80 NIS/day*

UNDERWATER OBSERVATORY MARINE PARK ★ ●

One of Eilat's major attractions 9km (6mi) south of the town in the direction of the Egyptian border. You can enter into the mysterious, colourful world of marine fauna and flora 100m from the shore and nearly 6m (20ft) below the surface of the water – without getting your feet wet. The Observatory also has several pools on dry land – with sharks, sea turtles, rays and other species – as well as an 'Oceanarium' where visitors can watch films that make them feel that they are in the depths of the sea (Sat–Thu 8.30am–5pm, Fri 8.30am–4pm | www.coralworld.com | entrance fee 89 NIS).

Another wonderful way to experience the underwater world of Eilat is on board the glass-bottom boat 'Coral 2000'. Mon–Sat 11am and 1pm | 20-min. cruise 50 NIS | tel. 08 6 33 35 60 | Coral Beach, 6km (4mi) to the south (bus line 15)

FOOD & DRINK

There are a great number of restaurants in Eilat in all price categories. The restaurants in the large hotels are among the most expensive but you can eat for less in the area around the Rechter Commercial Center.

INSIDER TIP THE FOOD FAIR

This is where the hungry find the best, and largest, buffet in Eilat. Daily 7am–10.30am and 7.30pm–11pm, in winter 6.30pm–11pm | in the Dan Eilat Hotel at the lagoon | tel. 08 3 66 22 22 | Moderate

GREEN ONION

Café, restaurant, milk shop. Popular place for young people to meet. Daily 8am–midnight | Bridge House | North Beach Promenade | tel. 08 6 37 74 34 | Budget

HALLELUYA

A mixture of biblical and Chinese food, prepared following kosher rules; the kitchen has received many awards. Daily noon–10pm | Tourist Center, in the Edomit Hotel | tel. 08 6 37 57 52 | Moderate

INSIDER TIP THE RED SEA STAR ☺

Underwater restaurant and pub on the floor of the Red Sea, 8m (26ft) below the surface. Imaginative complex where the owner, marine biologists and the National Park authority have established a 'Coral School' to protect the animals. Daily noon–midnight | opposite the Meridien Hotel | tel. 08 6 34 77 77 | www.redseastar.com | Moderate

SHOPPING

The Ha Yam Mall on North Beach between Mizrayim Road and the beach has the widest selection (daily 9.30am–midnight).

SPORTS & ACTIVITIES

Of course, the main focus in Eilat is on watersports – especially snorkelling and diving. The Coral Beach Nature Reserve (daily 9am–5pm | tel. 08 6 37 68 29 | www.parks.org.il | entrance fee 23 NIS) about 800m from the Underwater Observatory at a protected section of the coast, is ideal for snorkelers. Flipper and snorkel hire: 1 hour, 10 NIS. Another good address for watersports fans is the Red Sea Club with diving courses and boat tours lasting several days (Bridge House, North Beach | tel. 08 6 33 36 66 | www.redseasports.co.il).

ENTERTAINMENT

The hotspots in Eilat's nightlife are in the large hotels; e.g. the Platinum Disco in the Isrotel King Salomon Hotel and Ha Nesiha in the Princess Hotel (admission from 50 NIS). The *Dolphin Reef* organises large beach parties 3 times a week *(Mon, Thu, Fri | 25 NIS)*. And, *The Three Monkeys* next to the Royal Beach Hotel on the promenade has 2 large dance floors (outside and indoors) and live music every night after 9pm.

WHERE TO STAY

Overview of the hotels in Eilat: *Eilat Hotel Association | tel. 08 6 33 80 34 | www. eilathotels.org.il*

DAN EILAT

Well-maintained, modern hotel for families on North Beach; spacious, stepped building. Generous pool area, varied sports and entertainment possibilities. Children can spend the whole day in the Dannyland Children's Club in the neighbouring Dan Panorama Eilat Hotel. *378 rooms | tel. 08 6 36 22 22 | www.danhotels.com | Expensive*

HILTON QUEEN OF SHEBA

One of the best addresses in Eilat, impressive hotel complex with three swimming pools, spacious rooms and great comfort. *442 rooms | Northshore | Aritib Road 8 | tel. 08 6 30 66 66 | www.eilathilton.com | Expensive*

YOUTH HOSTEL

Large, attractive youth hostel at a central location only 100m from the beach. *500 beds, 13 double rooms | Arava Rd. 7 | tel. 08 6 37 00 88 | eilat@iyha.org.il | Budget*

INSIDER TIP ▶ PRINCESS ✼
Exclusive beach hotel with fantastic architecture, an oasis in the midst of a rocky landscape far from the hustle and bustle of Eilat, 8km (5mi) to the south. *355 rooms, 64 suites | Taba Beach (bus line 15) | tel. 08 6 36 55 55 | www.eilatprincess.com | Expensive*

INFORMATION

The public tourist office has been closed. Private organisations provide information online or in brochures available free of charge in hotels: e.g. *Eilat Guide | www. eilathotels.org.il* or *www.goisrael.com*.

EN GEDI

(125 E3) (*∭ E8*) En Gedi was once a biblical oasis; since 1950, it has been a kibbutz and today 100 people live here. Close to the 6700-acre nature reserve of the same name.

Until 1967, the Jordanian West Bank started to the north of En Gedi and it was only possible to reach the kibbutz from the south. A boom set in after the conquest of the West Bank and the construction of the new road from the Red Sea to Jerusalem. The kibbutz soon became famous for its therapeutic mud baths and sulphur springs. However, with the decline in the level of the Dead Sea, most of that has disappeared. En Gedi has an interesting nature park and still fascinates with its location on the shore of the Dead Sea. Coming from Jerusalem, visitors first reach the entrance to the nature park and youth hostel and then the turnoff to the kibbutz 2km (1¼mi) further south. The kibbutz itself and its botanical garden are close to the Dead Sea. A footpath in the nature reserve leads along a stream to *David's Waterfall*. National park visits: *daily 8am–5pm, Oct–March 4pm | entrance fee 23 NIS*

WHERE TO STAY

BEIT SARAH GUESTHOUSE

Youth hostel at the entrance to Nahal David. *51 rooms | tel. 02 5 94 56 80 | www. eingedi.co.il | eingedy@iyhc.org.il | Moderate*

THE SOUTH

EN GEDI COUNTRY HOTEL
The bungalow complex in the kibbutz with 85 large rooms has furnishings that have seen better days. However, the garden with its swimming pool, the food and the bar still make this a pleasant place to stay. *Tel. 08 6 59 42 20 | www.eingedi.co.il | Moderate*

FIELD SCHOOL HOSTEL ☙ ☺
A hostel for the environmentally minded, directly behind the youth hostel, on the outskirts of the nature reserve. This was formerly used by the military but is now the base of SPNI, the largest nature conservation organisation in Israel. Lavishly renovated. *42 rooms | tel. 08 6 58 42 88 | Budget*

EN GEDI TOURISM
Tel. 08 6 59 42 30 | www.ein-gedi.co.il

EN BOQEQ (125 D5) *(ᗰ E8)*
This settlement, 35km (22mi) south of En Gedi at the southern end of the Dead Sea, is an accumulation of hotels concentrating on medical treatments and spas. The dozen large hotels with about 700 beds next to the curative waters in pollen-free air mainly attract the health-conscious and sun worshipers.

The *Le Meridien Dead Sea*, in the midst of barren, unspoilt scenery, is a luxurious place to spend the night. Spa complex, four restaurants. *577 rooms | tel. 08 6 59 12 34 | www.lemeridien.com | Expensive*

MASADA ★ ● (125 D4) *(ᗰ E8)*
The difficult-to-reach rocky plateau of Masada (Mezada) rises 450m (1500ft) above the shore of the Dead Sea 13km (8mi) south of En Gedi. Herod had an impregnable fortress constructed on this

Swimming surrounded by salt crystals without sinking: bathing in En Boqeq

600m-long and 300m-wide cliff between 37 and 4BC. After the destruction of Jerusalem, around 1000 Jewish rebels entrenched themselves here. Only after a siege of 2 years was it possible for the Romans under General Flavius Silva to take Masada in 73AD; to achieve this, he built a mighty, long ramp of blocks of rock and earth on the west – which is still useable today. In order to avoid being enslaved, all of the besieged Jews decided to commit suicide following a stirring speech by their leader El Azar. This is how the Jewish-Roman historian Flavius Josephus depicted the events. Masada and the conviction of these radical religious nationalists, the Zealots, have great symbolic significance for Israel. The country's soldiers swear an oath of allegiance that 'Masada shall never fall again!'

The fortress, which was excavated in 1963 and magnificently restored, has been a Unesco World Heritage Site since 2001. There are 3 ways to get to the top: on foot, like the Romans, up the ramp on the west starting in Arad (around 2 hours); by walking up the 'snake path', which begins at the lower terminal of the cablecar on the eastern side and winds its way up the slope (about 45 mins.); with the *cablecar (Sun–Thu 8am–4pm, Fri 8am–2pm, every 20 mins. | return fare 72 NIS incl. entrance | www.parks.org.il, www.mfa.gov.il)*.

Son et lumière shows telling the story of Masada are held from *April–Aug: Tue, Thu at 9pm (Sept, Oct: Tue, Thu at 7pm) | entrance fee 45 NIS* (access only via the road from Arad). Accommodation is available at INSIDER TIP *Masada Youth Hostel* south of the plateau *(88 rooms, including 15 singles and 14 doubles | tel. 08 5 94 56 22 | massada@iyha.org.il | Budget)*.

QUMRAN
(125 E2) (*ka E7*)

This village that everybody started talking about in 1947 is on the northwest shore of the Dead Sea 30km (19mi) north of En Gedi. That is where the Palestinian shepherd boy Muhammed Adh-Dhib, from the Bedouin Ta'amirah clan, discovered jugs with the oldest Bible scrolls in a cave, completely by accident. The seven scrolls (including Isaiah texts) from the 1st century BC are now in the *Shrine of the Book* in the Israel Museum in Jerusalem.

Members of the Essene sect lived in Qumran in the years around the beginning of the Common Era. One of them – according to some researchers – might have been Jesus. The ruins of their monastery that the Romans destroyed in 67BC and the caves above it have been declared a national park. There is a visitors' centre at the entrance. A film introducing the life of the Essenes and documenting the history of the scrolls is shown in its air-conditioned rooms. *Sat–Thu 8am–5pm*

LOW BUDGET

▶ If you feel like you need a very good, inexpensive burger with salad and chips at any time between 7am and midnight, try the *Black Bar'n Burger (Napha St. 52)*. Strangely enough, it is opposite McDonald's.

▶ The *Timna Park*, on the N90 between the Dead Sea and Eilat 40km (25mi) before your reach the resort town, is a landscape full of natural wonders including fascinating sandstone formations and historical excavations (antique copper mines, temples, etc.). You will need 1–3 hours for the signposted thematic paths. *Daily from 7.30am–sunset | free admission*

(Oct–March 8am–4pm) | tel. 02 9 93 63 30 | www.parks.org.il | entrance fee 30 NIS

DEAD SEA ★ ●
(125 E2–4) (𝄞 E7–8)

It seems hard to believe that it is actually possible to lie on the surface of the water of *Yam Hamelah el-Bahr al-Mayyit* without going under. 10 times the amount of salt biblical cities of Sodom and Gomorrah were once located on the southwest shore before the Lord destroyed them as described in the Old Testament. An impressive pillar of salt here still reminds visitors of Lot's wife. The 'Dead Sea Industries' extract salt, bromine and – above all – magnesium south of Zohar Junction. Small and large floes of pure

Qumran: ancient scrolls were discovered in eleven caves like this one

normally found in seawater makes this possible, but it also makes it impossible for any life to exist in this inland lake. Around 80km (50mi) long, 3.5km (2mi) – 17km (11mi) wide, up to 400m (1300ft) deep in the northern section but not even 10m (35ft) deep in the south, divided in the middle by the Jordanian Lashon Peninsula – this is the geographical data of the Dead Sea. It is 394m (1290ft) below sea level, making it the lowest, accessible spot on earth.

The border to the Kingdom of Jordan runs exactly through the middle of the sea. The sodium chloride can be seen floating everywhere near the shore. Rainwater has washed out fascinating caverns (e.g. the *Arubotaim* and *Flour Caves*) in the neighbouring *Sodom Salt Mountains* stretching to the west. A visit to them is a desert adventure you will never forget. *www.deadsea.co.il*

The air is rich in oxygen and pollen-free, the minerals in the water are excellent for curing skin diseases, rheumatism and arthritis and this has led to *En Gedi* and especially *En Boqeq* developing into spas with modern treatment centres.

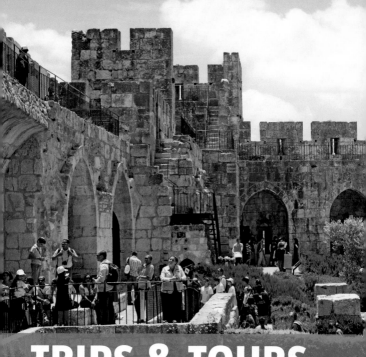

TRIPS & TOURS

The tours are marked in green in the road atlas, the pull-out map and on the back cover

1 JERUSALEM: FROM
JAFFA GATE TO THE
WESTERN WALL

This walk takes you through the sections of the Old City of Jerusalem that are steeped in history and contain places sacred to three religions: the Western Wall, the Dome of the Rock and the Church of the Holy Sepulchre. The tour begins at Jaffa Gate, passes through the Armenian Quarter and to the important sites outside the city walls on nearby Mount Zion. After that, we go to the Jewish Quarter and end at the most famous structures in Jerusalem: the Western Wall and the two mosques on the Temple Mount. You will need about half a day for this tour.

The historical centre has been surrounded by a wall that is up to 12m (39ft) high and 4m (13ft) thick since the 16th century. Sultan Suleiman – 'The Magnificent' – had it built partly on the foundations of Byzantine and Herodian sections of wall, between 1535 and 1540. 7 magnificent city gates lead into the Old City; the eighth has been closed for centuries.

After the British mandate, Jerusalem was part of Jordan until it was conquered and occupied by Israel in 1967. Today, it is divided into four quarters named after the communities living there near their reli-

Photo: Jerusalem: the citadel at Jaffa gate

Fascinating adventures in the Holy Land – experience Jerusalem's cultural variety and visit places mentioned in the Bible

gious centres – Christian, Jewish, Moslem and Armenian. The largest is the Arab Quarter (Haram Es Sharif) with the Temple Mount, the two large mosques and the bazaars. The Jewish Quarter, to the west of the Western Wall, was restored after 1967 and is now the most beautiful section. There are many monasteries, churches and institutions catering to pilgrims in the Christian Quarter. The Armenian Quarter is the most peaceful of the four. Most visitors staying in West Jerusalem enter the Old City of Jerusalem through Jaffa Gate. It was widened in the 19th century and later became famous when Emperor Wilhelm II rode through it in 1898, followed in 1917 by General Allenby. In former times, everybody who wanted go to Jerusalem's harbour on the coast, to Jaffa, left the city through Jaffa Gate.

The Israelis have created a connection between the mighty citadel on the right of the gate and King David – which is why it is now known as **David's Citadel** → p. 70 or the *Tower of David*. After you leave the citadel, you will be on Armenian Orthodox Patriarch Street. It is the most important thoroughfare in the **Armenian Quarter** → p. 70. Follow it until you arrive at the Armenian **St James' Cathedral** → p. 70. You will notice an Aramaic inscription on the wall as you enter the church. It states the believers worshipped in this church shortly after the Temple in Jerusalem was destroyed. It is said that the Virgin Mary was baptised in the stone font covered with silver.

The Armenian Quarter is a place of tranquillity and contemplation. There is no trace of the hustle and bustle that is so typical of the Christian Quarter. Going behind St James, you pass the **Armenian Museum** → p. 70 and, turning left, arrive at the city wall and Zion Gate.

Zion Gate was completed in 1540 during the regency of Sultan Suleiman – the Arab builder had the year and name of the ruler chiselled into the masonry. Several important places for Christians and Jews lie immediately to the south of the gate, outside the city wall, on Mount Zion.

When you pass through Zion Gate, which the Arabs call David's Gate *(Bab Nabi Daoud)*, you first reach the **King David's Tomb** → p. 70, a rock grave covered with velvet. During Shavuot celebrations, Jewish pilgrims leave you in no doubt as to its authenticity. Steps in the same building lead down to the **Cenaculum** → p. 70. This is the name given to the room in which Christians (with the exception of the Syrian Orthodox Church) believe that Jesus and his disciples celebrated the Last Supper. On the other side of the road, **The Chamber of the Holocaust** → p. 70 memorial site pays homage to the Jewish victims of

National Socialism. In dignified silence, Torah scrolls saved from a European synagogue, an eternal flame, and the names of the Jewish communities eradicated by the Nazis symbolise the indescribable magnitude of this crime. A little further to the west, nestled into the slope, the church of **St Peter in Gallicantu** → p. 70 recalls the place where Peter denied Christ.

You now return to the walled Old City through Zion Gate. Turn right, go past the large carpark on Tiferet Israel Square, turn left onto Hayehudim Street ('Street of the Jews') and go down to **Cardo** → p. 73. This is the heart of the **Jewish Quarter** → p. 73. In the Roman-Byzantine era, Cardo was the main street in Jerusalem and cut through the city from Damascus to Dung Gate. The shops inserted in the niches under the arches of the covered street still remind us of the history of this district.

Among the interesting sights in this quarter, the archaeological **Wohl Herodian Quarter Museum** and the so-called **Burnt House (Kathros House)** → p. 72, a reconstructed, restored home from the 1st century, deserve special attention.

Follow the signs up steps and through narrow streets until you reach the **Western Wall** → p. 73, the most important and sacred of all the Jewish sites. Before visiting the wall, why not pay your respects to Raghib Rishew in *Friends Restaurant (daily 11.30am–7pm | Western Wall Street 98 | tel. 02 6 27 39 01)*. In addition to humus and falafel, he also serves 'Oriental & Grilled Items' – delicious and inexpensive! The closer you get to the wall, the easier it will be for you to see the letters and notes to the Almighty stuck into the mortar-less cracks between the stone blocks. Only men and boys are permitted to enter Wilson's Arch from the northern end of the wall. Women and girls reach the arch and this section of the wall

The symbols of world religions: the Western Wall, the Al Aqsa Mosque, the Dome of the Rock

through special entrances above the forecourt but have to stay in the small niches on both sides of the row of arches, hidden behind curtains from the eyes of the men. Wilson's Arch is part of a wide Herodian bridge that joined the Jewish Quarter with the Temple Mount.

There is a wooden bridge to the right of the Western Wall over which tourists can reach the Al Aqsa Mosque and Dome of the Rock → p. 68 on the Temple Mount. If you would like to add another attraction to this walk, you can cover part of the distance on top of the Old City wall with the INSIDER TIP *Ramparts Walk (Sun–Thu 9am–4pm, Fri 9am–2pm | www.pami. co.il)*. There are stairs up to the ☀ coping of the wall at several city gates. For ex-

ample, this allows you to walk from Jaffa to Zion Gate and watch life in the quarters of the Old City going on below you, as well getting a good view of East Jerusalem beyond the walls through the battlements and embrasures.

2 AROUND THE SEA OF GALILEE

This tour begins and ends in Tiberias, the largest, best-known city in Galilee that stretches over the slopes on the western shore of the lake. The tour makes a wide arch around the biblical lake, passes places that became famous through Jesus and also gives you the possibility to take a swim.

If you want to lengthen the tour or spend more time bathing on this 71km (44mi) route, you should plan on spending a night in one of the kibbutzim. The shore of the Sea of Galilee is rocky so don't forget your flip-flops!

The Israelis also jokingly call their Yam Kinnereth a 'sea' when talking about the largest inland lake in the country. Its location in the Jordan Valley at the foot of the Golan Heights has fascinated people for thousands of years. The lake itself is the major attraction; the towns and villages on its shore are only interesting because of their location. No matter from where

and after 8km (5mi) arrive in Hamat Tiberias → p. 59 with its very attractive bathing possibilities that have existed since Roman days. Today, there are several public beaches and a large water park that will appeal to children. Further south, at the place where the River Jordan flows out of the southwest corner of Yam Kinnereth, you should visit the ● INSIDER TIP baptism complex in Yardenit that the Kinneret Kibbutz set up 'close to where Jesus was baptised' – that's what the sign at the entrance says. Following in the biblical tradition of John the Baptist, who baptised Jesus in the Jordan, single

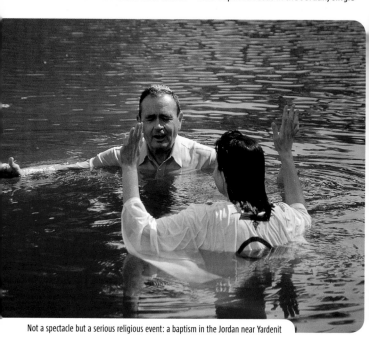

Not a spectacle but a serious religious event: a baptism in the Jordan near Yardenit

you look, the lake always seems to take on a different appearance.

You leave the historically important town of Tiberias → p. 58, which the Israelis call Teverya, on Highway 90 towards the south

or group Christian baptisms are performed here in the open air every day. The kibbutz also runs an enormous shop selling religious articles where you will be able to purchase a crown of thorns or blessed water from the Jordan as souvenirs and also rent (US $10) or buy (US $25) the obligatory white baptismal robe. Depending on your religion, you can hire a 'Baptist' ($60) and have a video made of the ceremony *(daily 8am–5pm, last baptism 3pm | Yardenit Baptismal Site | tel. 04 6 80 91 00 | www.yardenit.com)* Immediately after Yardenit, you reach the Deganya Kibbutz. This was founded in 1910 and is considered the oldest in Israel. It also has an outstanding scientific library. Route 90 turns south towards Jericho and the Dead Sea at the southernmost point of the Sea of Galilee → p. 63. From here (Zemah Junction), take Route 92 along the eastern shore of the lake. Route 98 branches off 8km (5mi) after this junction and takes you towards the Jordanian border and Hamat Gader, a recreational centre on the Yarmuk River, before heading up to the Syrian Golan Heights.

Route 92 on the eastern shore of the lake passes through the luxuriant banana and vegetable plantations that belong to the kibbutzim established here for strategic purposes. One of the most famous is located directly on the Sea of Galilee; En Gev → p. 61, where you can swim, relax or spend the night. Drive past the Kursi National Park on the northeast shore of the lake, where Jesus healed two farmhands minding their pigs who were possessed by the devil (Matthew 8:28–34), until you reach Capernaum *(Kefar Nahum)* on the north of the lake. Before this, you will have turned off Route 92 onto Route 87 from the Golan Heights at Yehudiya Junction and crossed the Arik Bridge over Jordan River where it enters the Sea of Galilee.

Capernaum → p. 62 is one of the most important places related to Jesus' life. This is where He healed lepers and madmen (Matthew 8:1–4, 16f) and a captain's servant (Matthew 8:5–13), where He visited the house of Peter (Matthew 8:14–17), recruited the first disciples (Matthew 8:18–22) and calmed a mighty storm crossing the lake (Matthew 8:23–27). Some of the buildings in Capernaum make reference to these miracles. Immediately to the west of Capernaum, directly on the lake, a large flat rocky plateau, the so-called Mensa Christi, recalls the third appearance of Jesus after his death when he ate with the disciples and named Peter his successor (John 21:1–25). Only 500m further to the west on Route 87, you will arrive at Tabgha → p. 63, in the midst of a luxuriantly green landscape, where Jesus fed the 5000 (Matthew 14:17–21). And, only a couple of miles away, the ☓ Mount of Beatitudes → p. 61, where Jesus held the Sermon on the Mount (Matthew 5:1–7) rises up over the plain. The best way to reach the Mount of Beatitudes is on Route 90 (Route 87 joins Route 90 at the Capernaum Intersection; from here, drive 2.5km (1½mi) to the north and follow signs on the right). You have the most beautiful panoramic view of the lake from the top.

If you now follow Route 98 along the western shore of the lake to the south, you will reach the Ginossar Kibbutz → p. 62, with its guesthouse *(68 rooms | tel. 04 6 79 21 61 | Moderate)* after a few miles. In 1986, a 2000-year-old, 8m wooden boat was unearthed here. The painstakingly conserved vessel can now be admired in the Yagal Alon Center in the kibbutz. Taking advantage of this find from Jesus' day, many of the tourist boats on the Sea of Galilee are now called 'Jesus Boats'.

Route 90 takes you straight back to Tiberias only 10km (6mi) away. If you would like to make a detour to visit the birthplace of Mary Magdalene, turn off towards the lake to Migdal after 5km (3mi).

SPORTS & ACTIVITIES

The Mediterranean climate enables many sports to be enjoyed throughout the year and sport is considered very important in Israel. Tourists can take join in many popular activities – it is even possible to go skiing in Israel, but only from December to February.

All large hotels have tennis courts and most of them also have a sports centre for their guests' personal fitness regime. But you will not have to rely on your hotel: there are many advertisements in the daily newspapers where health clubs praise their wide range of sports and training facilities with the latest fitness equipment. And you can hire a bike in all cities too.

Israel offers watersports enthusiasts – swimmers, yachtsmen, surfers and divers – excellent conditions. There are also first-rate events for those who prefer just to watch. Basketball is very popular; Maccabi Tel Aviv was European Champion twice. Information in the daily newspapers or from *The Israel Basketball Federation | Yehudit St. 36 | Tel Aviv | tel. 03 5 62 22 92 | www.ibba.one.co.il.* The Maccabi Haifa football club which won the Israeli championship 12 times, participates regularly in the European Cup. *www.maccabi-haifa.fc.walla.co.il*

The 'Jerusalem Post' publishes a monthly list of sporting events and facilities pro-

Israel is perfect for a variety of sports – golfing in Caesarea, riding in Galilee, kite surfing in Tel Aviv and diving in Eilat

vided by the *Israeli National Sports Association | Warburg St. 5 | Tel Aviv | tel. 03 29 63 87*.

BIRDWATCHING

Every year in March/April and Oct/Nov, Israel becomes an important stopover for migratory birds. The best places for birdwatching are in Galilee (e.g. in the Hule National Park) and on the Red Sea (e.g. in Eilat). Information: *International Birdwatching Center | Eilat | tel. 07 6 37 42 79* and *International Birdwatching Center of the Jordan Valley | Kfar Ruppin Kibbutz | tel. 04 6 48 06 12 | www.birdwatching.org.il*

DIVING

Sept–Dec and March–May are ideal for diving in the Mediterranean. If the water is calm, the range of vision can be over 10m (30ft) on a clear day, the tidal range averages 12 inches and the water temperature fluctuates from 16°C (61°F) in Feb to 27°C (81°F) in Aug. Information

The coral reefs off the coast of Eilat are especially well protected

and possibilities in Tel Aviv, along the coast and in the ancient harbour of Caesarea: *Scuba Dive Israel | tel. 054 4 94 65 23 | www.scubadiveisrael.com;* diving excursions to the Gordon Caves off the coast: *Dive Tel Aviv | tel. 054 6 62 70 44 | www.divetelaviv.com*

You can snorkel every day of the year among the beautiful coral in the protected underwater world of Eilat and dive from the shore or a boat. There are no dangerous waves or currents and the tides are hardly noticeable. The range of visibility is 15–40m and sometimes even more. The temperature of the water is between 21°C (70°F) in Feb and 27°C (81°F) in Aug. There are signposted underwater routes. Snorkelling equipment can be hired, e.g. in Eilat: *Shulamit's Eilat Diving Adventures | Ha Tsaftsefa St. | tel. 054 4 75 85 25 | www.shulamit-diving. com. U-Dive | Coral Beach | tel. 08 6 37 60 15 | www.u-dive.org; Aqua-Sport (www. aqua-sport.com),* the largest and oldest diving school (since 1962) has branches in Eilat and Taba on the Sinai Peninsula.

GOLF

There are two golf courses in Israel. The oldest (opened in 1961) and best-known is on the outskirts of the old Roman harbour town of Caesarea. You can put close to the beach, not far away from the amphitheatre and aqueduct. The 72-par, 18-hole course is 6800m long and open all year round. The sandy ground makes it possible to play soon after heavy rainfall. *Caesarea Golf and Country Club | next to Hotel Dan Caesarea | tel. 04 6 10 96 00 | Green fee: Sun–Thu 460 NIS, Fri/Sat 520 NIS, Golf Cart 130 NIS*

Golf can also be played throughout the year on the 9-hole course at the *Gash Kibbutz (20 north of Tel Aviv on the A 2 | tel. 09 95 15 11 | www.gaashgolfclub.co.il).*

HIKING

The ⏱ INSIDERTIP Israeli friends of nature in the *SPNI – Society for the Protection of Nature in Israel* organise hikes, lasting one or more days, in particularly beautiful, remote areas in the Negev, near the Dead Sea, in Galilee and elsewhere in the country. *Sun–Thu 9am–2pm, Fri 8am–1pm | Nahlat Binyamin St. 85 | Tel Aviv | tel. 03 5 66 09 60 | www.teva.org.il*

RIDING

Those wanting to explore the Sea of Galilee on horseback should pay a visit to the hotel ranch INSIDERTIP *Vered Hagalil (tel. 04 6 93 57 85 | www.veredhagalil.co.il)* north of the lake near Khorazim on Route 90 towards Rosh Pina.

SKIING

The only skiing area in Israel is on the north-eastern slopes of Mount Hermon at an altitude of 1600–2100m (5300–6500ft). It is 40 miles from Tiberias. There is a wonderful ☀ view of the Golan Heights and over Galilee from the *Hermon*. The skiing season begins in mid-Dec and lasts to the middle of March. During this period, the upper slopes are usually covered with heavy, wet snow – sometimes to a height of over 2m (6ft). The lifts operate from 8.30am–3.30pm; the runs are of varying difficulty and the longest is 2.5km (1½mi).

Moshav Neve Ativ (Ramat Ha Golan | tel. 04 6 98 13 33) is the centre of the skiing region. For information on conditions: *tel. 04 6 98 13 33*. Accommodation is available in the nearby *Manarah Kibbutz* or in the guesthouses run by the *Vered Ha Galil* and *Kfar Ha Nassi kibbutzim (28 flats | tel. 04 6 91 48 70 | www.kfar-hanassi.org.il)*.

SWIMMING

Swimming is possible throughout the year in the Gulf of Eilat and the Dead Sea and, from March–Oct, along the Mediterranean coast and in the Sea of Galilee. Trained lifeguards man all public beaches and swimming is free of charge. The most famous beach is the one stretching for miles in Tel Aviv. It is kept spotlessly clean and has excellent tourist facilities (sunshades, loungers, etc.). Almost all large hotels also have a swimming pool and it is often possible for people not staying there to use the facilities for a fee. Public swimming pools can be found in *Tel Aviv (Gordon Swimming Pool | Kikar Atarim)* and *Jerusalem (Jerusalem Swimming Pool | 13 Emek Refaim)* and many other places. *All pools March–Oct 8am–6pm, July/Aug 8am –10pm*

TENNIS

Tennis is very popular in Israel. The *Israel Tennis Center* in Ramat HaSharon north of Tel Aviv has 16 all-weather courts with floodlights and training walls; reasonably-priced tennis lessons. *Ramat HaSharon | Kafar Hayarkon Junction | tel. 03 6 45 66 66 | www.israeltenniscenter.com*

WIND & KITE SURFING

There are surf centres at all of the seaside resorts along the Mediterranean coast and in Eilat that hire all the equipment you need from boards to surf shoes; some of them also organise courses.

So far, kite surfing has remained limited to the Tel Aviv area. 'Kiters' get together on two sections of the beach where professional training is also given: *Surf Point (north of the Dolphinarium)* and *Sea Center (Hilton Beach)*. Information on wind conditions: *www.windfinder.com/report/tel_aviv_ben_gurion*

TRAVEL WITH KIDS

Israel is well prepared to welcome young tourists because, as a rule, Israeli families have several children and enjoy travelling around their native country. That is why there are biblical zoos, swimming pools with gigantic water slides and children's menus wherever you go.

You should stay in one of the kibbutz hotels if you plan to visit excavation sites on a hot day. The kibbutzim always have excellent playgrounds, are never without a swimming pool, and their kindergartens will also take care of guest children.

There are half a dozen seaside resorts along with Mediterranean coast with special sections for children with playground equipment. Tel Aviv, Netanya and Nahariya are especially praiseworthy in this respect.

Of all the large cities in Israel, *Tel Aviv* caters best to children. There is not only a long beach (usually right in front of your hotel) with professional 'baywatchers' but also many lovely playground areass for the little ones, even on fashionable *Sheinkin Street (Ha Tiftufia in Sheinkin Gardens)*.

THE MEDITERRANEAN COAST

CHILDREN'S MUSEUM
(124 B1) (*ℳ C–D6*)

This is the place for those who love technology: a museum for children from 4–12 years of age in which they should touch everything and can perform experiments themselves. Expert personnel help the children who they take to the various experimental sections in small groups. Children under the age of 9 have to be accompanied by an adult. *Mifratz Shlomo St. 1 | Peres Park in Holon | Tel Aviv | Sun–Tue, Thu 9 and 11.30am, Wed 5pm–8pm, Sat and holidays 9.30am–1pm | www.childrensmuseum.org.il | entrance fee 62 NIS, children 40 NIS*

KIDS AT THE MUSEUM (122 A6) (*ℳ C6*)

Tel Aviv's largest art museum, the *Tel Aviv Museum of Art*, has tours especially for children and has also set up a small circus school where youngsters can learn some tricks. In addition, the museum organises several half-day events for children from 6–16 in the summer months. *King Saul St. 27 | Sat, Mon, Wed 10am–4pm, Tue,*

Israel is also a country where kids feel at home – there are special offers for families, not only in kibbutzim

Thu 10am–10pm, Fri 10am–2pm | www.tamuseum.com, www.ilmuseum.com | entrance fee 25 NIS, children free

INSIDER TIP MINI ISRAEL
(124 C2) (*ɒ D6*)

This will interest the entire family: near Latrun, on the road from Tel Aviv to Jerusalem, the Tzora kibbutz has built a miniature, open-air version of Israel on a scale of 1:25. It is really fascinating to see all of Israel with its cities and important buildings (such as Jerusalem with the Western Wall, Haifa with the Baha'i Temple, or the skyline of Tel Aviv) as if you were Gulliver in Lilliput. This also gives children the opportunity to get an idea of the geographical dimensions and location of the cities. *Tzora Kibbutz | Sun–Thu 5pm–8pm, Fri 10am–2pm | www.mini-israel.co.il | entrance fee 79 NIS, children 59 NIS, audio guide 10 NIS*

JERUSALEM

BLOOMFIELD SCIENCE MUSEUM
(0) (*ɒ 0*)

This is a hotspot for families and their young Einsteins where they can make many, intriguing experiments. *Ruppen Blvd. | Givat Ram | Hebrew University | Mon–Thu 10am–6pm, Fri 10am–2pm, Sat 10am–4pm | www.mada.org.il | entrance fee 40 NIS (from the age of 5)*

THE TISCH FAMILY ZOOLOGICAL GARDENS (0) (*ɒ 0*)

All the animals in the Bible have been brought together in this 'Biblical Zoo' on the outskirts of Jerusalem. A real highlight: the Tiger Club with the baby tigers. *Manhat, near Malha Mall | bus 26, 33, 99 | Sun–Thu 9am–6pm, Fri 9am–4.30pm, Sat 10am–6pm | www.jerusalemzoo.org.il | entrance fee 47 NIS*

FESTIVALS & EVENTS

Israel's national weekly holiday is the Jewish Sabbath. It begins at sunset on Fri and ends on Sat evening, also when the sun sets. The weekly holiday for Moslems is Fri. Tourists will feel this in the Arab sections of Jerusalem and in the occupied territories. The Jewish calendar is based on the lunar cycle but is adjusted to the solar year with intercalary months so that the Jewish year always begins in autumn and the holidays always take place in the same season. The main Jewish holidays are also public holidays in Israel. In the case of Jewish celebrations lasting a week, the first day is a public holiday. All holidays begin at sunset on the night before.

JEWISH CELEBRATIONS

ROSH HA SHANAH
In the Jewish calendar, the creation of the world was in 3761BC. For devout Jews, ▶ INSIDER TIP ▶ *Rosh Ha Shanah* in 2012 marked the beginning of 5773. The ▶ *shofar* (curved ram's horn) is blown in synagogues to celebrate the New Year. Among the many traditional dishes eaten are honey cakes, grapes and slices of apple dipped in honey in the hope of a 'good, sweet year'. *17–18 Sept 2012, 4–5 Sept 2013, 25–26 Sept 2014, 14–15 Sept 2015*

YOM KIPPUR
The most sacred Jewish holiday; the Day of Atonement, of prayer and a day when all public activity comes to a standstill. *26 Sept 2012, 14 Sept 2013, 4 Oct 2014, 23 Sept 2015*

SUKKOTH
The Feast of Booths is the biblical harvest festival. In remembrance of the Children of Israel wandering through the desert, devout Jews spend time in huts made of branches and palm fronds in their front gardens or on their balconies. *1/2 Oct 2012, 19/20 Sept 2013, 9/10 Oct 2014, 28/29 Oct 2015*

SIMCHAT THORA
The end of Sukkoth is the day of 'Joy over the Torah' celebrated in processions and joint celebrations in halls. *8 Oct 2012, 27 Sept 2013, 17 Oct 2014, 6 Oct 2015*

The calendar is marked by the holidays of three religions, but especially Jewish festivals – the the high point being Yom Kippur

HANNUKAH
Festival of Lights commemorating the purification of the Temple by Judas Maccabeus. *8–16 Dec 2012, 28 Nov–5 Dec 2013, 17–24 Dec 2014, 7–14 Dec 2015*

PURIM
The return from captivity in Babylon is celebrated with parades, masquerades and a great deal of alcohol. *24 Feb 2013, 16 March 2014, 5 March 2015*

PESSACH (PASSAH, PASSOVER)
This is a week-long celebration in memory of the Jews' escape from Egypt. *26 March– 2 April 2013, 15–22 April, 2014, 4–11 April 2015*

YOM HA SHOA
Holocaust Remembrance Day. *6 April 2013, 26 April 2014, 11 April 2015*

YOM HA ATZMAUT
The day on which the independence of the State of Israel was proclaimed (14 May 1948). *16 April 2013, 6 May 2014, 23 April 2015*

SHAVUOT
The celebration of the revelation of God who presents the children of Israel with the Ten Commandments on this day. *15/16 May 2013, 4/5 June 2014, 24/25 May 2015*

FESTIVAL

ISRAEL FESTIVAL ⭐
The most important cultural event in the country: for three weeks in May and June, many foreign theatre, dance and music ensembles make guest appearances in Jerusalem and other parts of the country. *Tel. 02 6 23 70 00 | www.israel-festival.org.il*

LINKS, BLOGS, APPS & MORE

LINKS

▶ www.omanoot.com 'Omanoot' is the Hebrew word for 'art'. And that is why this young website, which is still under construction, has devoted itself to contemporary Israeli art (literature, cinema, music, fine arts)

▶ www.ddtravel-acc.com/travel.htm Practical information for your trip to Israel, incl. hotels, tours, city guides, holy places, museums, restaurants, etc. in all the main centre, plus other essention links incl. to government sites and general tourist information

▶ en.rsf.org/israel.html The homepage of Reporters Without Borders gives critical information on political developments in Israel and the region

▶ www.jerusalem.muni.il Official website of the City of Jerusalem. Extremely useful: 'Getting around' provides a list of all the tour guides approved by the Tourism Ministry

▶ www.972mag.com The magazine top journalists (from Ha'aretz, the Jerusalem Post, Calcalist and other media) are responsible for providing unbiased information and analyses of political events and developments

BLOGS & FORUMS

▶ israelisoldiersmother. blogspot.com The mother of two Israeli soldiers comments on current events in the conflict between Israelis and Palestinians. Her point of view is partisan and provocatively biased

▶ www.haaretz.com/blogs The Ha'aretz newspaper provides first-rate blogs with background information every day

Regardless of whether you are still preparing your trip or already in Israel: these addresses will provide you with more information, videos and networks to make your holiday even more enjoyable

▶ fromgaza.blogspot.com The Palestinian doctor and activist for human and women's rights, Mona El-Farra, reports from Gaza City

▶ http://vt.goisrael.com Virtual tour of Israels produed by the Israel Ministry of Tourism. Choose from a variety of itineraries (general interest/religion/culture)

▶ www.jr.co.il/videos/israel-videos.htm Compilation of many (currently 192) YouTube videos about Israel (Israel YouTube Playlist), organised in categories such as technology, cinema, history, religion, music etc.; most from a pro-Israeli viewpoint

VIDEOS & STREAMS

▶ Israel Weather This free app provides up-to-date weather forecasts from the Israel Meteorological Service

▶ Israel Tourism Users are provided with comprehensive, free information on tourist highlights. With GPS data and city maps

▶ Tzvi Ben-tzur In his short texts, Tzvi Ben-tzur uses postage stamps to give information on Israel and important personalities. The app is free

APPS

▶ www.wayn.com This is the right place for people interested in networking with globetrotters and Israelis. If you ask in the right way, you will get valuable information; if not, the tips are rather superficial. Of course, the activities of 'Wayn's friends' focus mainly on the tourist centres

▶ www.facebook.com/israelreise; www.facebook.com/goisrael Sites of the State Transport Office and Tourist Ministry. Information on tourist highlights, as well as performances and exhibitions

NETWORK

TRAVEL TIPS

ARRIVAL

The Israeli *El Al* airline *(www.elal.co.il)* and British Airways *(www.britishairways.com)* among others, fly several times a day between London and Tel Aviv Ben Gurion International Airport near Lod (24km/15mi southeast of Tel Aviv and 48km/30mi west of Jerusalem). Some flights are direct, others with stopovers and/or with other carriers. Charter companies operate direct flights to Eilat on the Red Sea. Airports: *www.iaa.gov.il.* Due to the different alternatives and flight times, it is worth spending some time comparing prices.

There are strict security controls before check-in and this makes it necessary to arrive at the airport around 3 hours before the scheduled departure time. Flying time from London to Tel Aviv is approx. 5 hours. Prices for a return flight start at around £500. Flight information in Tel Aviv: *tel. 03 88 11.*

RESPONSIBLE TRAVEL

It doesn't take a lot to be environmentally friendly whilst travelling. Don't just think about your carbon footprint whilst flying to and from your holiday destination but also about how you can protect nature and culture abroad. As a tourist it is especially important to respect nature, look out for local products, cycle instead of driving, save water and much more. If you would like to find out more about eco-tourism please visit: *www.ecotourism.org*

BANKS & MONEY

The currency is officially named the 'New Israeli Shequel' (NIS). The shekel is divided into 100 agorot.

Banks, hotels, post offices (reasonable) and exchange offices such as the one at *Damascus Gate* in Jerusalem (very reasonable) change money. Banks are open *Sat–Thu 8.30am–12.30pm* and. *4pm–5.30pm, Fri 8.30am–noon.* It is possible to change back NIS up to a value of US$500/£300 in the departure hall of the airport without any formalities. Credit cards are accepted everywhere and you can also withdraw money from cash dispensers using your EC card.

BED & BREAKFAST

There are around 8000 guest rooms in rural districts of Israel that are subsidised by the Ministry of Tourism and provide an excellent alternative to hotels. See: *www.zimmeril.com*

BUSES

Buses are the most used and cheapest means of transportation – both in the cities and for cross-country travel (a trip from Tel Aviv to Ben Gurion Airport costs around 35 NIS). All important towns are served by the green *Egged buses (Petah Tikya | Bareket St. 4 | Tel Aviv | tel. 03 6 94 88 88 | www.egged.co.il).* Dan *(tel. 03 63 94 44 | www.dan.co.il)* is the cooperative responsible for Tel Aviv. With only a few exceptions, all buses run from 5am–11.30pm (except on the Sabbath). Information at all central bus terminals *(Tahanal Merkasit).*

From arrival to weather

Holiday from start to finish: the most important addresses and information for your trip to Israel

CAR HIRE

It is not expensive to hire a car in Israel (from 150 NIS per day), cheaper if booked before leaving home. All international companies have offices at Ben Gurion Airport but charge an additional 95 NIS airport tax. The person hiring the car must be over 21 years of age, have a national or international driving license (issued at least 12 months before), passport and credit card (as security).

CUSTOMS

You may take the following with you to Israel: presents up to a value of £200/US$300, 200 cigarettes, 1 litre of spirits, 10 films. It is forbidden to import meat, fruit and weapons. The duty-free limits for articles from Israel which can be taken back to the EU are: 200 cigarettes, 1 litre of spirits, 50g of perfume and presents up to a total value of £350.

Travellers to the US who are residents of the country do not have to pay duty on articles purchased overseas up to the value of $800, but there are limits on the amount of alcoholic beverages and tobacco products. For the regulations for international travel for US residents please see *www.cbp.gov*

DRIVING

It is fun to drive in Israel: the dense network of roads is well looked after. It is compulsory to wear seatbelts and the following speed limits apply: 50km/h (30mph) in built up areas, 80km/h (50mph) on national roads and 90km/h (56mph) on motorways.

Alcohol limit: 0.0%. Traffic and information signs are usually in three languages (Hebrew, Arabic and English). Stopping is

BUDGETING

Snack	£1.60/$2.60
	for falafel with salad bought on the street
Coffee	£1.60/$2.60
	for a cup of coffee in a restaurant
Oranges	40p/¢70
	for 1 kilo in summer
Bus	80p/$1.30
	fare in the city
Petrol	90p/$1.40
	for a litre of unleaded super
Museum	up to £4/$6.50
	admission

permitted at the blue-and-white marks on the kerb, forbidden at the red-and-white ones and your car will be towed away immediately if you stop in a red-and-yellow area. A litre of super petrol costs around 8 NIS.

Emergency and towing service is provided by the Israeli Automobile Club *MEMSI, Headquarters: Memsi House | Harakevit St. 20 | Tel Aviv | tel. 03 5 64 11 11 | www.memsi.co.il*

ELECTRICITY

220 V alternating current. Power points differ so take an adapter with you.

CURRENCY CONVERTER

£	NIS	NIS	£
1	6.10	10	1.50
3	18.50	30	5
5	31	50	8.50
13	80	130	22
40	250	400	65
75	460	750	125
120	740	1200	200
250	1540	2500	415
500	3080	5000	825

$	NIS	NIS	$
1	3.80	10	2.50
3	11.50	30	7.50
5	19	50	12.50
13	49.50	130	32.50
40	152	400	100
75	285	750	187.50
120	455	1200	300
250	950	2500	625
500	1900	5000	1250

For current exchange rates see www.xe.com

EMBASSIES & CONSULATES

BRITISH EMBASSY IN TEL AVIV
1 Ben Yehuda Street | Migdalor Building, 15th Floor | Tel Aviv 63801 | tel. +972 37 25 12 22 | ukinisrael.fco.gov.uk/en

BRITISH COUNCIL IN PALESTINIAN TERRITORIES
31 Nablus Road | P.O. Box 19136 | Jerusalem 97200 | tel. +972 26 26 71 11 | www.british council.org/ps

EMBASSY OF THE UNITED STATES OF AMERICA
71 Hayarkon Street | Tel Aviv 63903 | tel. +972 35 19 74 75 | israel.usembassy.gov/

EMERGENCY SERVICES

Police: tel. 100; Magen David Adom (Red Cross): tel. 101; Fire Brigade: tel. 102

HEALTH

Medical care in Israel is excellent. All doctors speak English. Foreigners must pay their bills immediately in cash or by credit card; for this reason, it makes good sense to take out heath insurance for abroad.

IMMIGRATION

Citizens from the UK, US, Canada, the EU and many other countries do not need a visa, but your passport must be valid for at least 6 months. If you intend visiting an Arab country (with the exception of Jordan and Egypt) at a later date, you must be sure that there are no Israeli stamps in your passport. You should inform the border official that you do not want to have an Israeli stamp in your passport. Foreign tourists can travel to the Palestinian administered territories at any time; the Israeli government forbids Israelis to do this. Tourists may stay in the country for up to three months. This can be extended at any of the *District Offices of the Ministry of the Interior* in the major cities.

INFORMATION

MINISTRY OF TOURISM
www.goisrael.com

INTERNET

Useful internet addresses to help you plan your stay: *www.embassyofisrael. co.uk* (site of the Israeli Embassy in the UK with general, as well as political, economic and cultural, information); *www.*

jerusalem-hotels.org.il (website of the Jerusalem Hotel Association).

INTERNET CAFÉS & WIFI

Almost all hotels, Christian hospices and youth hostels offer their guests internet access. There are also internet cafés in all cities, e.g. in Tel Aviv: *Private Link (Ben Yehuda St. 78 | tel. 03 5 29 98 89 | 1 hour 40 NIS)*; in Eilat: *Unplugged Bar (Tourist Center | tel. 08 6 32 62 99 | 30 mins. 20 NIS)*; in Jerusalem: *Eye Tech (Old City, near New Gate | tel. 02 6 26 42 61 | 1 hour 25 NIS)*.

There are some isolated WiFi hotspots in Israel. These are in all expensive hotels (at a charge!) and a few cafés in large cities (free!). Comprehensive, free coverage: *Sheinkin Street* in Tel Aviv. For an overview see: *www.hotspot-locations.com*

KIBBUTZ GUESTHOUSES

There are kibbutz hotels throughout the country; most are bungalow complexes in beautiful surroundings that belong to the individual kibbutzim and their comfort makes them comparable with good standard category hotels *(Budget–Moderate)*. Information and reservations: *Kibbutz Hotels Chain | Smolanskin St. 1 | Tel Aviv | 61031 | P.O. Box 3193 | tel. 03 5 24 61 61 | www.kibbutz.co.il*

NEWSPAPERS

There are around two dozen Israeli newspapers but the conservative 'Jerusalem Post' and left-wing liberal 'Ha'aretz' are the only two published in English. Ha'aretz is the only newspaper critical of the government and includes a supplement from the International Herald Tribune.

USEFUL PHRASES HEBREW

Yes/No	ken/loh	כן/לא
Please/Thank you	bevakasha/todah	בבקשה
Excuse me/sorry!	sleexa!	סליהה!
Hello!	shalom!	שלום !
Goodbye!	lehitrahot!/lehit!	להתראוח להח !
My name is ...	schmi ...	שמי ...
I don't understand you	anee loh meveen/a otcha	איני מבין/נהאוחך
How much is it?	kama zeh oleh?	כמהזהעולה?
What time is it?	ma hasha-a?	מההשעה?
I would like to ...	anee mevakesh ...	אני מבקש ...
I (don't) like that	zeh (loh) motzeh xen be einei	וה(לא) מוצאהן בעיני
Where can I find ...?	heichan yesh ...	היכן יש ...?

0	efess	אפס		
1	achat/echad	אחח/אחר	20 esrim	עשרים
5	chamesh/chamisha	חמש/חמישה	21 esrim ve-echad	עשרים ואחר
10	eser/assara	עשר/עשרה	100 meah	מאה
			101 meah ve-echad	מאהואחר

NUDE BATHING

Bathing without a swimsuit, or even topless, is not permitted in public and frowned upon.

PHONE & MOBILE PHONE

Telephone cards are needed for making calls from public phones. They can be bought in all post offices and in many shops; the cards have varying amounts of credit (from 20 NIS). You can choose the most economical provider for foreign calls by replacing the second '0' of the dialling code with a specific number: currently, the cheapest way to telephone to Europe is by dialling *013* or *014* (1 min. approx. 5 NIS).

British mobile phones work everywhere in Israel but the roaming fees charged by the Israeli providers are extremely high. Prepaid cards are expensive but they save on roaming fees. Texting is always cheap. Your mailbox can cause high costs: turn it off before you leave home! You can always rent a second mobile phone with the appropriate SIM card and new telephone number any time at the airport in Tel Aviv. Mobile phone companies are next to each other in the arrival hall.

POST

The logo of Israeli post offices is a white deer on a red background. They are open *Sun–Thu 8am–12.30pm and 3.30–6pm, Fri 8am–noon.* Postcards to Europe 3 NIS; letters 4.50 NIS.

TAXIS

Taxis in Israel are less expensive than in the UK. City taxis have a taximeter and it is compulsory to use this. If the driver suggests turning it off, it will hardly ever be to your advantage. Tips are accepted. There are fixed rates for cross-country travel; the drivers have a list for you to inspect – e.g. Tel Aviv – Ben Gurion Airport costs 70–100 NIS.

Sherut taxis operate in and between most important cities. The taxis set off when they have enough passengers. Cross-country trips start at the central bus terminal; in Jerusalem, near Zion Square. Tel Aviv–Ben Gurion Airport costs around 30 NIS.

TIME

GMT plus 2 hours. Israel also has daylight saving time; this is not the same as in Europe but in keeping with the Jewish calendar.

TIPPING

Tipping is a matter of course in Israel. A service charge is not always included on a restaurant bill. If this is the case, it is still expected (between 10–15%).

TRAINS

There is only a modest railway network, e.g. from Tel Aviv via Haifa to Akko or south to Ashdod, into the Negev Desert to Beersheba and to Dimona, and between Tel Aviv and Jerusalem. The modern stations are outside city centres. *Tel Aviv: Al Parashut Derachim St., Jerusalem: New Station, Yitzhak Modai, Malcha | timetables and prices: www.rail.co.il*

VAT

Prices of all goods purchased in Israel include 17% VAT. If the amount is more than £30/$50, the *Bank Leumi* at the airport will issue an export certificate upon presentation of the bill and the VAT will be refunded to tourists leaving the country (fees: £3/$5, £5/$8 above £60/$100).

is green and the temperature hardly rises above 25°C (68°F).

WEATHER, WHEN TO GO

Israel is a year-round destination but there are considerable variations in climate from region to region; for example, Jerusalem, in the mountains at an altitude of over 800m (2500ft), has dry, warm summers and cold winters – sometimes it even snows. However, in general, winters in Israel are mild, both on the Mediterranean coast and in the Negev Desert and Eilat. The Jordan Valley and Dead Sea are hot and dry in summer. The most pleasant time is March–May when the countryside

YOUTH HOSTELS

There are currently 18 youth hostels in Israel that are united in the *Israel Youth Hostel Association (IYHA)*. An overnight stay, including breakfast and bedding, costs £10–18/$15–30; there are also double rooms. No age limit. Maximum stay, 21 days. It is not necessary to have a youth hostel ID and this will not even bring you a discount. Bookings: *IYHA | Binyanei Ha'mah, International Convention Center | Jerusalem | Shazar St. 1 | tel. 02 6 55 84 00 | www.iyha.org.il*

WEATHER IN TEL AVIV

	Jan	Feb	March	April	May	June	July	Aug	Sept	Oct	Nov	Dec
Daytime temperatures in °C/°F	18/64	19/66	21/70	23/73	26/79	28/82	30/86	31/88	31/88	28/82	24/75	20/68
Nighttime temperatures in °C/°F	8/46	9/48	11/52	13/55	16/61	19/66	21/70	22/72	21/70	17/63	14/57	11/52
Sunshine hours/day	6	7	7	9	11	12	12	12	10	9	8	6
Precipitation days/month	10	8	8	2	0	0	0	0	0	4	6	10
Water temperatures in °C/°F	16/61	16/61	17/63	18/64	21/70	24/75	25/77	27/81	27/81	24/75	21/70	18/64

NOTES

FOR YOUR NEXT HOLIDAY ...

MARCO POLO TRAVEL GUIDES

ALGARVE
AMSTERDAM
AUSTRALIA
BANGKOK
BARCELONA
BERLIN
BRUSSELS
BUDAPEST
CALIFORNIA
CAPE TOWN
  WINE LANDS,
  GARDEN ROUTE
COLOGNE
CORFU
GRAN CANARIA
CRETE
CUBA
CYPRUS
  NORTH AND
  SOUTH
DUBAI

DUBROVNIK &
  DALMATIAN COAST
EDINBURGH
EGYPT
FINLAND
FLORENCE
FLORIDA
FRENCH RIVIERA
  NICE, CANNES &
  MONACO
HONGKONG
  MACAU
IRELAND
ISRAEL
ISTANBUL
JORDAN
KOS

LAKE GARDA
LANZAROTE
LAS VEGAS
LONDON
LOS ANGELES
MADEIRA
  PORTO SANTO
MALLORCA
MALTA
  GOZO
MOROCCO
NEW YORK
NEW ZEALAND
NORWAY
PARIS
RHODES

ROME
SAN FRANCISCO
SICILY
SOUTH AFRICA
STOCKHOLM
TENERIFE
THAILAND
TURKEY
  SOUTH COAST
UNITED ARAB
  EMIRATES
VENICE
VIETNAM

- PACKED WITH INSIDER TIPS
- BEST WALKS AND TOURS
- FULL-COLOUR PULL-OUT MAP
  AND STREET ATLAS

ROAD ATLAS

The green line ▬▬ indicates the Trips & Tours (p. 96–101)
The blue line ▬▬ indicates The perfect route (p. 30–31)

All tours are also marked on the pull-out map

Photo: Caesarea Maritima

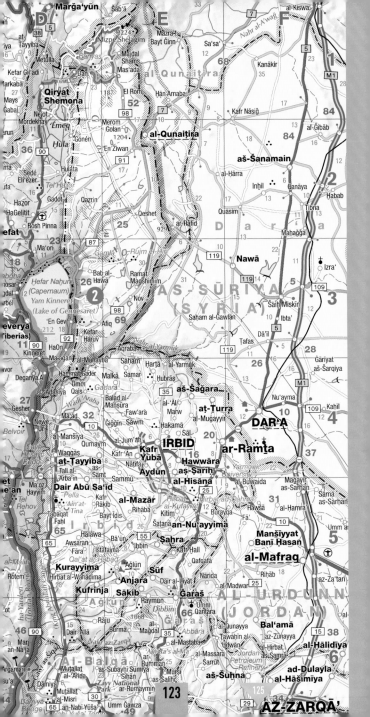

A

10 km
6.2 mi

Mediterranean

Sea

RAMAT GAN **PETAH TI**
TEL AVIV-YAFO Giv'atayim Qir. Ono
BAT YAM Yehud
HOLON Or Yehuda 20
RISHON LE ZIYYON Lod
Ramla
Palmahim 431
Nes Ziyyona **REHOVOT** Mo
Yavne Mazkeret Batya
Gedera 23
Tel Mor 48
ASHDOD Revadim
Mayki'im Qiryat Tirosh
Mal'akhi **Bet Sheme**
29 Kefar Menahem Rama Shem
Berekhya Agur Li On
ASHQELON Negba 67 Zafririm Afia
Ozem 40
Tel Ashqelon Nehora Bet Guvrin
Yad Mordekhay 13 35 Bet Guvrin
Qiryat Gat Tel Maresha Tarqu
Bayt Helez Even Idna
Bayt Hanina Shemu'el Tel Lakhish
Lahiya Lakhish
GAZZA Tel Hasi Ahuzzam Amazya
GABALIYA Sederot 7 Negohot
Nuşeirāt Yakhini al-Majd
Sa'ad Duma
Dair al-Balah Mabbu'im Bet Qama ad-Dāhiriya
al-Bureij Shomeriyya
Gazza Mugazi Devira
HĀN Kissufim Re'im **Netivot** Rahat
YŪNIS Bani Şuheila 50 Mishmar Lahav Tene Shi
Nirim Berosh HaNegev Metar
Tall Rafah Magén 40 Hura Tel
RAFAH Urim **Ofaqim** Éshel Yeshu
Rafah 30 234 HaNasi 'Omer
Sufa Hazerim Tel Be'ér Sheva
Kerem Yesha **BE'ÉR SHEVA**
Sadot Shalom Gevulot Nevatim
Ze'elim 25
222
Y Horvot Haluza 260 309 Horvot Aro'er
I Horvot Rehovot 222
S (BaNegev) Revivim
304 **R** Mash'abbé 224
372 Sade Yeroham
Ashalim
A 39 211 Horvot Haluqim
Nizzana Sedé Boqer 433
Kezziot Horvot Shivta Midreshet Ben Gurion
79 31 En 'Avedat
126 **124**
Gabal al-Sabha 449 'Ezuz Horvot 'Avedat

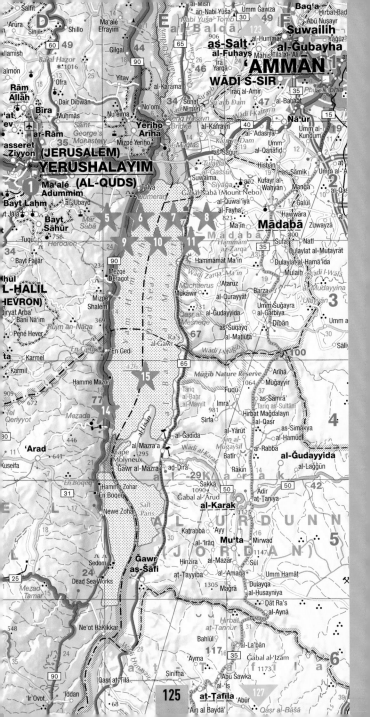

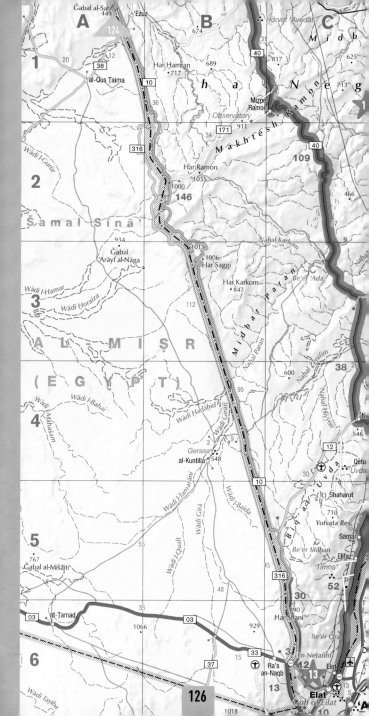

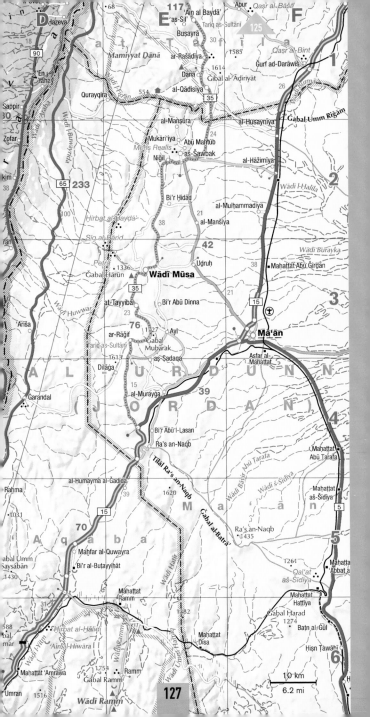

D | Hazeva
90
18
V | 'En Yahav
Sappir
30
Zofar
kim
38

'Abur | Qaṣr al-Bāšā
68 | **117** 'Ain al Baydā' | **E** aṣ-Ṣīl | **F**
Ṭarīq aṣ-Ṣultānī | **125**
Buṣayrā
30 | at-Ṭefīla
Mamiyyat Dānā | ar-Rašādiya | 1585 | Qaṣr al-Bint | **1**
Dānā | 1614 | Gurf ad-Darāwīš
Gibāl al-'Ādiriyāt
al-Qādisiya | 26
Qurayqira | 554 | al-Qādisiya
35 | Gabal Umm Riġām
al-Manṣūra | al-Ḥusayniya
24
Mukāri'iya | Abū Maḥtūb
Melis Realis | aš-Šawbak
Niġil | al-Ḥāzimiya | **2**
65 | **233** | Wādī l-Ḥalila
Bi'r Ḥidād | al-Muḥammadiya
Hirbat al-'Baydā' | 21 | al-Manšiya
38 | **42**
Sīq al-Bārid | Wādī Burayka
Petra | 1336 | Udruḥ | 38 | Maḥaṭṭat Abū Girḍan
Gabal Hārūn | **Wādī Mūsa**
35 | 21
at-Ṭayyiba | Bi'r Abū Dinna | 15 | **3**
23 | ✝
'Arīša | 76 | 1727 | Ayl | **Ma'ān**
ar-Rāġif | Gabal Mubārak
Ṭarīq aṣ-Ṣultānī | 1613 | aṣ-Ṣadaqa | Asfar al-Maḥaṭṭat
Dilāġa | **A** | **L** | **–** | **U** | **R** | **D** | **U** | **N**
15 | al-Murayġa | **39**
Garandal | **(** | **J** | **O** | **R** | **D** | **A** | **N** | **)**
Bi'r Abū l-Lasan | **4**
Ra's an-Naqb
Tilāl Ra's an-Naqb | Maḥaṭṭat Abū Ṭarafa
Rahma | al-Ḥumaymā al-Ġadīda | Wādī Bayir Nū Ṭarafa
39 | Wādī š Šīdiya
1620 | **M** | Maḥaṭṭat aš-Šīdiya
1031 | **a** | **a** | **n** | 5
15 | Ra's an-Naqb | Gabal al-Batrā' | 1435 | **5**
A | **70** | **q** | **a** | **b** | **a** | 1261
bal Umm | Maḥfar al-Quwayra | Qal'at aš-Šīdiya | Maḥaṭṭa Abbat
Saysābān | Bi'r al-Buṭayyiḥāt
1430 | Maḥaṭṭat Ḥaṭṭiya
Maḥaṭṭat Ramm | Gabal Harad
1382 | 1274 | Baṭn al-Ġūl
588 | Hirbat al-Ḥālieḥ | Wādī Ḥaṭīm | Ḥiṣn Ṭawābī
bal 'Ain al-Hiwāra | Wādī Ramm | Maḥaṭṭat Disa | **6**
mar
Maḥaṭṭat 'Amrāwa | 1754
Umran | 1516 | Ramm | Gabal Ramm | **10 km**
Wādī Ramm | **127** | 6.2 mi

KEY TO ROAD ATLAS

18 26	Motorway with junctions Autobahn mit Anschlussstellen
=====	Motorway under construction Autobahn in Bau
I	Toll station Mautstelle
⊙	Roadside restaurant and hotel Raststätte mit Übernachtung
⊛	Roadside restaurant Raststätte
⊛	Filling-station Tankstelle
═══○═══	Dual carriage-way with motorway characteristics with junction Autobahnähnliche Schnell- straße mit Anschlussstelle
═══════	Trunk road Fernverkehrsstraße
───────	Thoroughfare Durchgangsstraße
───────	Important main road Wichtige Hauptstraße
───────	Main road Hauptstraße
───────	Secondary road Nebenstraße
───────	Main line railway Fernverkehrsbahn
🚗	Car-loading terminal Autozug-Terminal
───────	Mountain railway Bergbahn
•○•○•○•	Aerial cableway Kabinenschwebebahn
++++++	Chair-lift Sessellift
....	Railway ferry Eisenbahnfähre
🚗	Car ferry Autofähre
-------	Shipping route Schifffahrtslinie
───────	Route with beautiful scenery Landschaftlich besonders schöne Strecke
Alleenstr.	Tourist route Touristenstraße
×—×—×—×	Road closed to motor traffic Straße für Kfz gesperrt
8% ◀	Important gradients Bedeutende Steigungen
⊖	Check-point Grenzkontrollstelle
⊖	Check-point with restrictions Grenzkontrollstelle mit Beschränkung

✷ Observatory ✷ 'En Gedi	Of interest: culture - nature Sehenswert: Kultur - Natur
～～～	Bathing beach Badestrand
☀	Important panoramic view Besonders schöner Ausblick
☐☐☐	National park, nature park Nationalpark, Naturpark
░░░	Prohibited area Sperrgebiet
♠ ♣	Church, Monastery Kirche, Kloster
♦	Mosque Moschee
⋈ ⌂	Kasba, Tomb Marabout Kasbah, Maraboutgrabmal
♦	Palace, castle Schloss, Burg
♣ ♠ ♦ ♂	Ruins Ruinen
⚑ ♦	Lighthouse, Tower Leuchtturm, Turm
♉	Moorish castle Maurische Burg
▲ ∩	Cave, Monument Höhle, Monument
∴	Archaeological excavation Ausgrabungsstätte
⌂	Tourist colony Feriendorf
⬟	Isolated hotel Allein stehendes Hotel
▲	Camping site Campingplatz
🌴	Grove of palm-trees Palmenhain
✈ ✈	Airport, Regional airport Flughafen, Regionalflughafen
─··─··─	National boundary Staatsgrenze
─·─·─	Controversial boundary Umstrittene Staatsgrenze
～～～～	Full Palestinian civil and security control Palästinensische Autonomiegebiete 'A-Zonen'
JERUSALEM	Capital Hauptstadt
HAIFA	Seat of the administration Verwaltungssitz
▬▬▬	Trips & Tours Ausflüge & Touren
▬▬▬	Perfect route Perfekte Route
⭐	MARCO POLO Highlight

INDEX

This index lists all places and sights in this guide as well as important names and geographical terms. Numbers in bold indicate a main entry.

WRITE TO US

e-mail: info@marcopologuides.co.uk

Did you have a great holiday?
Is there something on your mind?
Whatever it is, let us know!
Whether you want to praise, alert us
to errors or give us a personal tip –
MARCO POLO would be pleased to
hear from you.
We do everything we can to provide the
very latest information for your trip.

Nevertheless, despite all of our authors'
thorough research, errors can creep in.
MARCO POLO does not accept any
liability for this. Please contact us by
e-mail or post.

MARCO POLO Travel Publishing Ltd
Pinewood, Chineham Business Park
Crockford Lane, Chineham
Basingstoke, Hampshire RG24 8AL
United Kingdom

PICTURE CREDITS
Cover photograph: Dome of the Rock and the cupola of St Mary's Church in Jerusalem (Huber: Szyszka); Doves (Getty Images/Flickr: Toussia-Cohen)
DuMont Bildarchiv: Argus (6, 45, 71, 106, 108/109); Eretz Hatzvi Event (16 centre); © fotolia.com: foodcolors (16 top); Getty Images/Flickr: Toussia-Cohen (1 top); G. Hartmann (2 centre top, 2 centre bottom, 2 bottom, 3 top, 5, 7, 9, 30 left, 30 right, 32/33, 54/55, 56, 63, 64/65, 77, 85, 95, 99, 100, 110 top, 110 bottom, 111); G. Heck (1 bottom); Huber: Schmid (10/11, 28, 34, 39, 41, 46, 61, 66, 72, 90, 93, 102/103, 120/121, 129), Szyszka (1 top); F. Ihlow (front flap left, 12/13, 18/19, 28/29); KOTIK PRECIOUS METAL: Guli Cohen (16 bottom); Laif: Amsler (104), Gerald (108), Kerrber (3 bottom, 96/97), Hilger (8, 58), Polaris (80), Shabi (83, 109); Laif/hemis.fr: Maisant (48, 51); Laif/Le Figaro Magazine: Martin (3 centre, 53, 86/87); Laif/REA: Kotz (27); Look: Fleisher (106/107); mauritius images: Alamy (24/25, 37, 107), Clasen (26 right), von Poser (2 top, 4, 26 left); La Terra Magica: Lenz (front flap right, 15, 20, 23, 29, 42, 69, 74, 79, 88); Philip Blau: Anatoly Michaelo (17 bottom); Rebooks: Dov Shechter (17 top)

1st Edition 2013
Worldwide Distribution: Marco Polo Travel Publishing Ltd, Pinewood, Chineham Business Park, Crockford Lane, Chineham Basingstoke, Hampshire RG24 8AL, United Kingdom. Email: sales@marcopolouk.com
© MAIRDUMONT GmbH & Co. KG, Ostfildern
Chief editors: Michaela Lienemann (concept, managing editor), Marion Zorn (concept, text editor)
Author: Gerhard Heck; editor: Nadia Al Kureischi
Programme supervision: Anita Dahlinger, Ann-Katrin Kutzner, Nikolai Michaelis
Picture editors: Gabriele Forst, Barbara Schmid
What's hot: wunder media, Munich
Cartography road atlas & pull-out map: © MAIRDUMONT, Ostfildern
Design: milchhof : atelier, Berlin; Front cover, pull-out map cover, page 1: factor product munich
Translated from German by Robert Scott McInnes; editor of the English edition: Christopher Wynne
Prepress: M. Feuerstein, Wigel
Useful phrases in cooperation with Ernst Klett Sprachen GmbH, Stuttgart, Editorial by Pons Wörterbücher

DOS & DON'TS

A few things you should bear in mind in Israel

DO RESPECT PEACE ON THE SABBATH

God rested on the seventh day and, in the Bible, He demands that people do the same. But, He asks for even more such as 'Ye shall kindle no fire throughout your habitations upon the Sabbath day' (Exodus 35:3). This is a strict commandment for devout Jews and they do not even smoke on the Sabbath. In many hotels, small cards on the tables remind absent-minded guests to respect this tradition. Exodus 35:3 also prevents Orthodox Jews from driving on the Sabbath because igniting the motor is a modern-day version of fire. The Mea Shearim district in Jerusalem is closed to all traffic on this day. The faithful do not want to be photographed at the Western Wall on the Sabbath and that should be respected – those affected will take matters into their own hands to prevent this.

DON'T BE DISAPPOINTED BY THE 'HOLY LAND' BUSINESS

It can be rather worldly in the Holy Land and especially at the holy sites! Profound religiosity and merciless fleecing – you will experience both at the same time. This is most obnoxious in Jerusalem and there, near the Church of the Holy Sepulchre: Crowns of Thorns in sizes S to XXL are offered as souvenirs and heavy wooden crosses can be hired for you to carry along the 14 Stations of the Via Dolorosa. And there is always a priest standing at Jesus' grave in the centre of the Church of the Holy Sepulchre with a discreetly extended hand waiting for a contribution. He gets it too; who would deny a humble servant of the Lord a token sum at His grave. But, it is important to know that, among the many Christian confessions represented in Jerusalem, only the six present in the Church of the Holy Sepulchre worked out a precise timetable for making these collections after centuries of heated quarrelling.

DON'T CHANGE MONEY AT BEN GURION AIRPORT

Tourists like to have the local currency as soon as they land so that they can make their first purchases right away. If at all, you should only exchange a small amount at Ben Gurion Airport because there you have to pay a special 'Airport Tax' in accordance with the amount you change – this is around 10 percent for 500 NIS – in addition to the regular fees.

DON'T USE THE LIFT ON THE SABBATH

There are several lifts in the skyscraper hotels. The Lord forbade work on the seventh day and that means that devout Jews cannot press the lift button on the Sabbath. In every hotel, one lift is coded to stop automatically at every floor from Friday evening to Saturday evening. If you take one of these lifts to your room on the 25th floor, it might take you up to half an hour.